>MATERIAL PROCESS

>YOUNG ARCHITECTS_4

>MATERIAL PROCESS

>FOREWORD/Billie Tsien and Tod Williams
>INTRODUCTION/Anne Rieselbach

>IS.AR IWAMOTOSCOTT
>L.E.FT
>MESH ARCHITECTURES
>DELLA VALLE + BERNHEIMER DESIGN
>J. MEEJIN YOON
>DZO ARCHITECTURE

>Princeton Architectural Press/New York
>The Architectural League of New York

>Published by
  Princeton Architectural Press
    37 East Seventh Street
      New York, New York 10003

>For a free catalog of books, call 1.800.722.6657.
  Visit our web site at www.papress.com.

State of the Arts

>The publication was supported in part with public funds from the
  New York State Council on the Arts, a state agency.

NYSCA

>Additional support provided by the LEF Foundation.

>Editor/Jennifer N. Thompson
>Series designer/Deb Wood
>Designer/Jan Haux

>Special thanks to: Nettie Aljian, Ann Alter, Nicola Bednarek, Janet Behning,
  Megan Carey, Penny Chu, Russell Fernandez, Clare Jacobson, Mark Lamster,
    Nancy Eklund Later, Linda Lee, Nancy Levinson, Jane Sheinman, Katharine Myers,
      and Scott Tennent of Princeton Architectural Press
        —Kevin C. Lippert, publisher

>Library of Congress Cataloging-in-Publication Data
>Young architects 4: material process/foreword by Billie Tsien and
  Tod Williams; introduction by Anne Rieselbach.
    p. cm.
>ISBN 1-56898-374-3 (pbk.: alk. paper)
>1. Young Architects Forum. 2. Architecture—Awards—United States.
    3. Architecture—United States—20th century. 4. Young architects—United States.
      5. Building materials. I. Title: Young architects four. II. Title: Material process.
        III. Architectural League of New York.
  NA2340 .Y6793 2003
  720'.79'73—dc21

                                        2002153336

>YOUNG ARCHITECTS_4
>MATERIAL PROCESS

>CONTENTS

>ACKNOWLEDGMENTS

>Wendy Evans Joseph//President/The Architectural League
of New York

>The League gratefully acknowledges the support that has made
this series and publication possible. Ongoing commitments from the
Greenwall Foundation, Artemide, Dornbracht, Miele Architects and
Designers Resource Group, and Tischler und Sohn and from
new sponsors A. E. Greyson & Company and Hunter Douglas Window
Fashions, continue to insure the success of the Young Architects
Forum exhibition, lectures, and web site installations.

>This publication would not be possible without the support of the LEF
Foundation, the New York State Council on the Arts, and the efforts
of the staff at Princeton Architectural Press.

>FOREWORD_I
>Billie Tsien

>I am sitting on a plane flying to Hong Kong thinking about the food I will eat when I get there. The itinerary I have for the next few days revolves around meals that are also meetings. Chinese life revolves around food. So does Chinese American life. When something good happens and I talk with my mother, she tells me to get something good to eat to celebrate. When something bad happens, she tells me to get something to eat so I will feel better. And of course it is important when serving food to guests that there is more than can possibly be eaten. I think this may be why I like ingredients so much.

Good meals are invented from ingredients. You don't have to invent the ingredients; you just have to put them together in an interesting way with a little tweaking.

One of the benefits of being an architect is the license to call up factories and ask to visit. Although it's not exactly the grocery store, it's a kind of foraging. Getting to see how things are made allows you to speculate on how they *might* be made. In our studio we love to take field trips to factories.

My earliest and one of my most memorable field trips took place in first grade. We went to a bread factory. I remember a machine that looked like a gigantic front-loading washing machine with a big glass door. Inside a huge wad of dough was bouncing around. It smelled wonderful. Pans with rising dough moved slowly by on conveyor belts, and at the end of the assembly line we were presented with a miniature loaf of bread. It was amazing to watch something you had always just thought *existed*—being made.

Not so long ago we made a field trip to visit the Endicott Clay Products in Fairbury, Nebraska. We were there to look at iron spot brick for a project at the Cranbrook Schools. The brown clay was simply dug from a pit nearby, mixed with oil, extruded from a square tube like the world's longest brownie mix, and sliced with a strand of wire.

The darker the brick, the longer it had been baked, just like brownies. As we were walking, I noticed a woman painting tiny little bricks. She was making samples of glazed brick. The ones I thought were the most beautiful were rejected because the glaze was too thin. These bricks showed the texture and the color of the original brick through a more transparent wash of color. I asked her whether they could make us bricks that were like the rejects and they did. These glazed bricks bring a wash of blue and green to the walls of an indoor swimming pool.

One doesn't need to invent ingredients. The time required for invention is indefinite and doesn't fit easily into a project schedule. Invention must be pursued sparingly if one is to work in the real world. But adaptation allows the sharing of the experience and knowledge of those who have had time to work out the problems with the addition of an outsider's perspective.

Ingredients are inspiring. Like going to the farmers' market in a foreign country—you don't need to know what you will do with the ingredients, but you feel inspired to try something.

As architects we are united in our love of the physical world. We like to touch and make real things. The work of the young architects shown in this book is particularly inspired by looking at real materials and the act of making real things. It is a wonderful meal.

>FOREWORD_II
>Tod Williams

>This year's theme of "Material Process" produced a great response from many interesting young architects. Had the theme been different, most of the winners would still have been selected for their multi-valent voices. Now is the time when these architects are developing clear voices and they should be heard.

A certain amount of (fleeting) fame—the lecture series and exhibition—is a product of the Young Architects Forum. The exhibition, extending a little over a month held in a small space, inevitably creates good will and energy, and remains a highlight. It is obvious that even as times change and new sensibilities challenge old, architecture is promise, is hope.

Architecture at a larger civic scale—be it the Sydney Opera House, the Eiffel Tower, or the Twin Towers—captures and symbolizes the culture and the public's imagination. Yet it is often an architect's small-est work that can affect people's lives most deeply. Within the past year the public has been moved to think deeply about their environment. Tall buildings have been vilified but this reactionary fear has been replaced by a new hope for a city that will be rebuilt, one with a soul and a spirit, where all people will find a home.

The winning architects have not proposed new cities. Their work is a close connection between hand and head. The projects emerge through long hours, the difficulties of the creative search, and yes, sim-ple toil. The materials they use—plywood, computers, metal, light—are not exotic. The results are intended to be experienced and touched, and to record our aspirations at this time.

We must rebuild our cities. It will take time, and I hope these and other young architects will play an important part. Small-scale passionate work speaks volumes. It is the touchstone of our daily existence. May architects' voices remain young, and let us appreciate those who proceed with vigor, a positive spirit, and integrity.

>INTRODUCTION

>Anne Rieselbach

>Since 1981 the Architectural League's Young Architects Forum has recognized the work of talented architects and designers still young in their careers. Selected through a nationwide competition, participants in the Young Architects Forum win the opportunity to present their work to their peers and the design community at large through an exhibition, lecture, web installation, and this publication.

Each year a committee of young architects, selected from past competition winners, develops a theme reflecting current issues in architectural design and theory. They also ask prominent members of the design community to serve with them on the competition jury. In 2002, in addition to committee members Thaddeus Briner, Mimi Hoang, and Chris Perry, the jury included Paola Antonelli, Wendy Evans Joseph, Sheila Kennedy, Gregg Pasquarelli, and Tod Williams.

The 2002 competition theme, "Material Process," was developed in response to the Architectural League's year-long program initiative "Fabricating Architecture." Each entrant was asked to analyze how his or her work related to the theme, which was intended both to examine construction—with an emphasis on new or reinvented building materials—and the means of making design into form, particularly through direct fabrication methods enabled by new digitally linked technologies.

For the exhibition at the League, winners must translate the work illustrated on their portfolio pages into a multidimensional display. Each year their installations have grown in complexity and sophistication. This may be due, in part, to previously prohibitively expensive or inaccessible technology that has become increasingly available to architects willing to take on the challenge of learning new methodologies. Many examples of digitally fabricated design elements, used to create functional and often elegant structures, were featured in the exhibition.

Another part of today's revised design equation is a change in the basic elements of construction. Materials research, along with new fabrication technologies, has enabled architects to envision uses for a new palette of building materials, as well as to reimagine uses for more traditional materials. In the hands of young architects these new applications have very often been used to change the nature of interior space. Just as another generation of architects created, albeit with very solid walls and contrasting voids, the notion of "open plan," today's young architects are calling into question traditional readings of interior space. Using means such as translucent, blurred, undulating, or kinetic dividers that are sometimes further dissolved through embedded light and exposed information systems, they seem to translate virtual space into three dimensions.

Lisa Iwamoto and Craig Scott of IS.Ar: IwamotoScott attempt to "balance exploration in digital processes and media modeling of prototypes, and hands-on material research with investigations into perceptual and experiential phenomena." They develop their designs with laser-cut and digital models, material studies, and more traditional handmade models and renderings. The Faculty Resource Room at the University of Michigan, designed using three-dimensional modeling programs, mixes a tactilely rich collection of simple materials such as MDF, particle board, cast rubber, liquid applied epoxy flooring, and sheet vinyl. Other projects, such as a series of digitally generated furniture studies and prototypes, allow experiments with materials and production at a smaller scale. The Fog House in Marin County exemplifies another ongoing theme in the firm's work: the idea of transformation between solid and void. The relationship of the house to the landscape and the perceptual vagaries implicit in the often fog-blanketed environment, create an ambiguous relationship between material presence and implied form.

>**INTRODUCTION**

>Anne Rieselbach

An Alucobond wall, water jet–cut directly from a computer file, displayed the work of Elena Fernandez, Arnaud Descombes, Antoine Regnault, and David Serero, the partners of DZO Architecture. Its shimmering form expressed the sinuous and inventive quality of their work. The material (a lightweight composite made of rubber sandwiched between two layers of aluminum) both carried applied signage and, when folded, supported architectural models. Many of the firm's projects incorporate components created through computer numerically controlled (CNC) devices, either through the direct milling of parts such as freeform wavelike "wood furniture-walls" or the creation of foam molds for casting. Three-dimensional modeling software also gives form to ongoing experimentation with the "fusion of structure and program." For example, in (UN)-SCRIPTING, the firm's entry for the Flemington Jewish Community Center design competition, DZO Architecture abstracted Hebrew calligraphy to generate spatial forms and literally wrapped the building's exterior with text.

Eric Liftin's installation was partially constructed from a number of remnants and materials from his firm Mesh Architectures' built commissions with virtual fields of information carried on computer screens. Twin panelite screens, composed of honeycomb aluminum paneling faced with acrylic, framed a freeform fiberglass wall fragment designed using a three-dimensional computer-modeling program. One computer controlled a series of diffused colored LED lights set behind the translucent panel, an animating detail that Liftin has incorporated in his work. The projects, a series of lofts, commercial spaces, product designs, and web sites, could be viewed on one of two flanking LCD panels. The composition and construction of the installation reflected Liftin's goal to integrate the realms of virtual and real space. His firm's web site designs display a three-dimensional reading of layered information. Their architectural commissions appropriate and translate digital fields—either through embedding them directly in the architecture or by creating similar shifting planar layers capable of transforming space by their translucent nature or by their movement.

Four spare strips of images displayed the work of Jared Della Valle and Andrew Bernheimer of Della Valle + Bernheimer Design. This straightforward presentation gave form to their pragmatic design philosophy: "solve a problem by solving a problem." Comprised of a series of digital prints face-mounted between aluminum and Plexiglas, the narrow strips were floated from the wall surface by aluminum supports. Composed as storyboards, they documented three projects—the Federal Plaza renovation in San Francisco, the P.S. 18 library renovation in Staten Island, and an artist's loft in Boston—from conception to completion, with an emphasis on the construction process. Thus, the architects presented the building process as a linear production, as opposed to the often circuitous design process. The firm looks to "a kind of invention in familiarity" to create designs that "make new things out of those that are both intimately and vaguely familiar." In both the artist's loft and the library renovation, sculptural steel walls, incorporating storage and display, bisect the open space to create more intimate zones of occupation.

J. Meejin Yoon's work has centered on "the mutability of materials and their technologies with respect to the body and its material envelopes: skin, clothing, and architecture." Yoon's kinetic installation reflected the sensibility of the work created within her hybrid practice as an author, educator, and architect. The Interactive Pleated Wall utilized CAD-CAM (computer-aided design/computer-aided manufacturing) technology to create an interactive aluminum display wall. Cut and perforated on a water-jet cutter, aluminum panels were hinged together to create a folded surface that ranged in depth, gaining in structural stability as the folds created more depth. Stacked vertically, light boxes were held within the folds, drawing the observer closer to the wall. A body's approach was detected by an infrared sensor, which signaled a circuit board, designed in collaboration with Matt Reynolds, to activate a series of rods that retracted to reveal Yoon's work. Alongside the wall was another sensor-activated piece, the Defensible Dress, which raised prickly spines when approached.

The work of Makram el-Kadi, Ziad Jamaleddine, and Naji Moujaes, the partners of the design collaborative L.E.FT, is devoted to speculative projects that "investigate the intersections of cultural and political productions." Their work exploits and subverts elements of the everyday within domestic space and in commercial projects best defined as "gathering spaces." L.E.FT's installation employed fairly pedestrian elements in a tantalizingly irrational way that literally tripped visitors and compelled them to explore the work. Reversing readings of floor and ceiling, floor-mounted light fixtures made of bent steel held "down-up" shades and a fluorescent bulb. Each shade carried montages of the firm's work including One Door House, a plan generated by a central revolving door, and Home Sweet's Home, an addition for a suburban house that "understands the house as a cross section through Sweet's catalogs," offering a collection of off-the-shelf products to create a "deluxe ordinary" house.

Much of the work that came out of Fabricating Architecture, while grounded in material exploration and expression, also possessed a quality of physical and conceptual transformation. Young architects have moved beyond an earlier design generation's explorations of the possibilities of computer-generated design, which, for lack of a direct means of production, often remained solely in a two-dimensional realm. Designers now can take for granted the computer's role as a tool both for design and production. The resulting one-off customized components are often used in tandem with almost aggressively everyday off-the-rack materials, to create places and spaces that purposefully contrast the unique with the familiar. The decorative and space-making potential of often irregular computer-generated volumes and light-transforming new materials is frequently used to shape a new kind of multifunction live/work space, efficiently and artistically creating permeable boundaries for multiple aspects of daily work and life.

>BIOGRAPHIES

>**IS.Ar IWAMOTOSCOTT** was formed in 1998 and is located in Berkeley, California. Lisa Iwamoto teaches in the Department of Architecture at UC Berkeley, and Craig Scott teaches in the Architecture Department at California College of Arts & Crafts in San Francisco. Iwamoto has a bachelor of science degree in structural engineering from the University of Colorado, Boulder and a master of architecture degree with distinction from Harvard University. Scott has a bachelor of architecture degree from Syracuse University and a master of architecture degree with distinction from Harvard University.

>**L.E.FT** is a design collaborative comprised of architects Makram el-Kadi, Ziad Jamaleddine, and Naji Moujaes. Established in New York City in 2001, L.E.FT is dedicated to examining the intersections of cultural and political productions as they relate to the built environment. With an interest in diverse programs, a focus on unconventional interpretations of the ordinary is posited as a design onset. All three partners received their bachelor of architecture degrees from the American University of Beirut. el-Kadi received his master of architecture degree from Parsons School of Design, Jamaleddine from the Harvard University Graduate School of Design, and Moujaes from SCI-Arc.

>Eric Liftin received his bachelor of architecture degree from Yale University and his master of architecture degree from Columbia University. He worked at New York architecture firms Bernard Tschumi Architects, Butler Rogers Baskett, and Resolution: 4 Architecture then joined the Internet startup Firefly Network in 1996 as an interface architect. He founded **MESH** Architectures (http://mesh-arc.com) in 1997. Liftin was a fellow at Harvard's Berkman Center

for Internet and Society. He currently teaches in the Interactive Telecommunications Program, the art and technology program at New York University.

>Jared Della Valle received his bachelor of arts degree from Lehigh University in 1993 and his master degrees in both architecture and construction management from Washington University in St. Louis in 1995. He worked for Clark Construction in New York City prior to founding **DELLA VALLE + BERNHEIMER DESIGN**. Andy Bernheimer received a bachelor of arts degree from Williams College in 1990 and his master degree in architecture from Washington University in St. Louis in 1994. He worked at Kohn Pedersen Fox and the Gleicher Design Group prior to founding Della Valle + Bernheimer Design. He currently teaches as a visiting architecture critic at the Rhode Island School of Design.

>**J. MEEJIN YOON** is currently an assistant professor in the Department of Architecture at the Massachusetts Institute of Technology. She established an interdisciplinary design practice in 2001. Her current design research investigates the intersections between the body, clothing, and architecture. She holds a bachelor of architecture degree from Cornell University and a master of architecture in urban design degree from the Harvard University Graduate School of Design, and she was a Fulbright grant recipient in 1997.

>**DZO ARCHITECTURE** (http://www.degrezero.com) was founded in 1998 in Paris and New York City by architects Arnaud Descombes, Elena Fernandez, Antoine Regnault, and David Serero. DZO has won several architecture awards including the French Nouveaux Albums des Jeunes Architectes in 2001. In 2002 DZO was selected to be part of the French Pavilion at the eighth Venice Biennale.

>IS.AR IWAMOTOSCOTT

>MATERIAL/PHENOMENAL_PHENOMENAL/MATERIAL

>IS.Ar aims to exploit particular properties and intensities of space and matter by approaching the design process as an ongoing exploration into questions of materiality and perception—often in flux, mutable, self-organizing. While tackling the given concerns of program, form, and constructability, our work proceeds along multiple, simultaneous lines of inquiry: investigation through digital media, iterative and speculative modeling of physical prototypes, and empirical study of experiential and perceptual effects of material with hands-on design research.

In attempting to engender an architecture that can engage the complex spatial and temporal dynamics of everyday life, certain touchstone ideas resurface and are revisited. These include: schematic potentials of the void as organizer of surrounding matter; configurational possibilities of the transformative whole over the fragmentary or too-clear articulation of parts; experiential value of perceptual instabilities, shifting appearances; economy-of-means implications of density of experience versus density of matter; constructive allowances and sponsorships of change over time; and the questioning of particular assumed distinctions, such as between surface and solid, landscape and building, or high and low technologies.

>SURFACE THICKNESS

>Faculty Resource Room

>College of Architecture and Urban Planning, University of Michigan, Ann Arbor

>Given the many programmatic requirements that were specified for the small 550-square-foot space (model photography, copy stand, storage, computer lab, meeting space, slide storage, and lounge), it was necessary to think of how the room could be made spatially dense while allowing for a sense of collective space. We began to think of thickness as an operative term that could allow for a density of programmatic use and conceptually bracket the material research.

The programs are made legible through material surface and thickened space. The concept of spatial thickness is tied to the notion of creating multiple levels of interior within the room. Using the visual agenda of the project to call out predominant areas, we sought materials that could both give visual depth and be responsive to particular programmatic needs. The project employs both constructional variation using computer numerically controlled (CNC) modeling of common and inexpensive building materials including particle board and medium-density fiberboard, as well as develops the sensuous possibilities of less conventional products such as cast rubber, liquid applied epoxy flooring, and sheet vinyl.

Capitalizing on the potential of the design-build process to amplify the dialog between the design's conceptual terms and its materials and methods of construction, we focused on the visual and tactile qualities of materials, and explored how they might be fabricated to gain certain qualities. Because we were ostensibly working with something as simple as a wall panel, we tested how the room liner might be made to reveal something about its materiality, use, or visual complexity. In our desire to maximize the performance of each surface, we welcomed unforeseeable material effects. It was these possibilities, opened up while translating

design concepts into material reality, that made the design-build
process an improvisational and speculative construction endeavor.

>Project team: Adam Clous, Timothy Wong, Daniel West, George Ristow,
Gerald Bodziak, John Commazzi, Anselmo Canfora

>**top_left/right**_>Luminous wall and desk made of sheet vinyl and perforated
aluminum. Perforated poché made of MDF.

>**bottom**_>Unfolded room plan

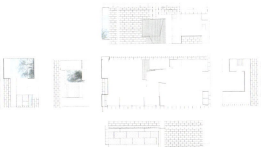

>**left**_>Exploded axon showing room liners
>**top**_>View through funnel
>**bottom/left**_>View through funnel
>**bottom/right**_>Laminated and warped funnel wall

>**top/left**_>View from back of room

>**top/right**_>Soft surface materials

>**bottom/left**_>Funnel details

>**bottom/right**_>Laminated construction funnel

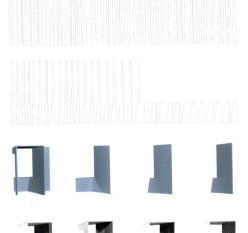

>CHAIR PROTOTYPES

>Two recent chair prototypes—spiral and noodle—yield further opportunities to engage in one-to-one scale research of symbiotic links between material and process. Both designs endeavor to generate spatial, optical, and formal effects that are amplified beyond the means of their construction.

>Project team: Carl Lorenz

>NOODLE CHAIR

>Noodle Chair is driven by a meshing between interests in perception and economy of means. The design investigates the potential of a bundle of repetitive modules of primary geometry transformed by a single cut. By looking at the particular geometries of a cut associated with the body in a sitting or lounging position, the chair reveals a hidden complexity of both material and module. The modules themselves are made with foam swimming-pool noodles—an inexpensive, familiar, and soft material—and held together with a perforated plastic inner rack resembling a six-pack can holder.

>**left**_>Internal "six-pack" noodle holder

>**right**_>Noodle layout and chair cutting planes

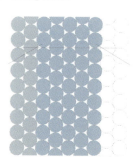

>**top**_>Texture of chair surface

>**right**_>Swimming-pool noodles

>**bottom**_>Chair, put together and unfolded

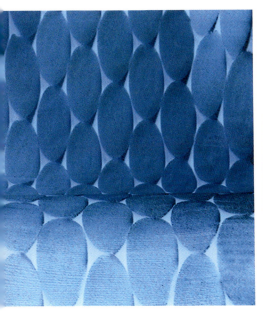

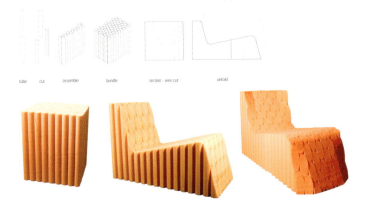

tube   cut   assemble   bundle   section - wire cut   unfold

>CHAIR PROTOTYPES
>SPIRAL CHAIR

>The spiral chair investigates relationships between digital modeling, computer-controlled production, and material research. The chair consists of three intersecting spirals. As the spirals are made from a single cut of material and together form a three-dimensional network, their geometric relationships are highly interdependent. This intertwining forms the conceptual basis for the chair.

The process began with a series of initial prototypes that investigate the correspondence among two-dimensional drawing, material thickness, and the resulting spiral forms. A process was eventually formed that employs three-dimensional modeling to carefully control the chair shape and find the intersecting geometries of the spirals. This data is then translated back into two dimensions to form material templates for laser or water-jet cutting. Through trial and error, initial prototypes of fiberglass-laminated plywood gave way to thinner and thinner aluminum. The three spirals are assembled and spot-welded (ultimately pressure-fitted) together at corresponding notches.

>**left**_>A bowl bought at a crafts fair in Mexico inspired the search for a three-dimensional object made with a minimal amount of cutting of flat material stock.

>**center**_>Early material study

>**right**_>Early model used to develop an armature along which a spiral can travel

>**top/left**_>Water jet–cut aluminum spirals

>**top/right**_>Study of a single spiral in a chair configuration and
study of interlocking spirals in a chair configuration

>**bottom/left**_>Full-scale prototype with vinyl seat pad

>**bottom/right**_>Seat shape derived from points of intersection

>FOG HOUSE

>Marin County, California

>This project seeks to engage the complex spatial and temporal dynamics of its situation through the formal and experiential activation of surface and landscape. It also attempts to blur the categories and definitions of both surface and landscape, such as between surface and solid, or landscape and building. The spatial quality derives from attempting to synthesize the specificity of the context with the particularity of the client's program brief—accommodating both private residence and home office for a biofeedback consulting practice in a new house.

Surface is used in this project as the medium to capture, reveal, and heighten latent, sometimes ephemeral, qualities present at the site. Located on the ridge between the Marin Headlands and the San Francisco Bay, the site occupies the near high point on the ridge from which it has access to 270-degree views. The panorama that wraps the house differs significantly on each side, and the perception and experience of the place changes as one turns and moves; San Francisco Bay to the east, Golden Gate Bridge to the south, Pacific Ocean to the west, and Mount Tamalpais to the north.

While revisiting a place in different seasons can often reveal dramatic differences, here the span of a few hours can exhibit an incredibly quick and dynamic transformation as fog rolls in from the Pacific Ocean and sweeps up the hillsides. The fog often blankets the surrounding lower landscape, making the site an island in the clouds, through which the Golden Gate Bridge's towers protrude, until they too are finally engulfed. This fog has a tangible presence, and it is possible to see it moving across objects in the landscape similar to how clouds appear from an airplane. The fog perhaps most clearly defines the corporeal presence of the site's phenomenal and unstable characteristics.

>**top**_>View toward ocean—day/afternoon

>**center**_>Concept diagrams

>**bottom/left**_>Groundworks informed by nearby hedge windbreaks, property line demarcations, and fog movement. Main living level organized by views.

>**bottom/left**_>View from road through fog void

Original volume of house | Void connecting primary views | Void creating fog access | Combined Voids

A driving concern for the project became how to directly and spatially engage such dynamic phenomena of view and fog. In response to the client's desire to be living in a "single story of a glass skyscraper," the initial diagram of the house is conceived as a simple glass volume, out of which site-generated voids are carved. Drawing initially from the topography, the ground surface is conceptually and materially stretched through the house to foster engagement with near and distant phenomena. The exterior of the original volume inflects to respond to the dynamics of the surrounding conditions. This volume also deforms to create particular alignments between internal spaces and adjacent edges such as between the eastern property line hedge and the courtyard terrace.

The house is organized around two overlapping voids, both created through an extension of interior and exterior landscape surfaces. This overlap is thought of as a condition of spatial double negative. One void, emerging from the hillside, funnels and harnesses the fog to effect a spatial redefinition of the interior. The second, beginning at the ground of the auto court and entry, is formed by a continuous surface that winds through the regular block volume as a way to fold together building and landscape, interior and exterior, and to further define internal spatial arrangements. The warped surface links diagonal spaces in the house, making it a viewing mechanism that conjoins the bay and ocean. This surface works its way upward to a roof garden, creating an artificial ground plane that recalls the auto court and offers a fully exposed perch among the elements.

The design is further developed as a hybrid combining figured earthwork (reminiscent of the nearby bunker architecture of the Marin Headlands) and the client's desired hovering glass box. In engaging the complexity of situation and program, these two paradigms interact to become a transformative whole. The interior formation of the voids is amplified by treating parts of the program as pochéd solids. These form a solid presence further defining

>**top**_>View from east looking toward Marin Headlands and Pacific Ocean
>**bottom**_>Cross section cut through fog void and through main living space

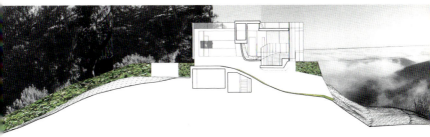

the cut space figures. At the same time, the spatiality of the house is both one of carved voids and of open, continuous surface. Both conceptually reference the ground and tie the glass box into the hill. Given the varying conditions of the view in different directions, the poché rooms are each distinguished by a particular landscape— Mount Talmapias in the master bedroom, the Golden Gate Bridge in the kitchen, etc.

Relationships of landscape to enclosure are intentionally made problematic in the Fog House. The interior nature of solid to void inverts with the presence of fog. On a clear day, the house acts diagrammatically like an open glass box, pulling distant landscapes deep into the interior and extending the view outward. The living space and family room unite across the terrace and allow the programs to function together. The two rooms often become separated, however, at times when low-visibility fog engulfs and splits the glass box's interior. The fog makes rooms, and the spatial diagram transforms into one of a set of carved and discrete spaces.

While it was our intention to suppress overtly legible tectonics in favor of a seamlessness of surface, certain distinctions are made that recall the relationship of earthwork to high-rise. The construction of the house employs a concrete groundworks out of which a steel frame structure emerges. The reading of the box is reestablished by a continuous glass enclosure, though it is again contested on the interior with the formation of fluctuating space, and through the skin's varying degrees of transparency and opacity.

>Project team: Je-Uk Kim, Tak Cheng Sze, Etienne Kuhn, Tonino Vicari

>**left/top**_>View from auto court toward entry

>**left/bottom**_>View from living room

>**right**_>top: Lower-level plan, bottom: Upper-level plan

>**bottom**_>Views through courtyard terrace without and with fog

>LOOP HOUSE

>Clear Lake, Michigan

>Loop House is an adaptation of a modest 1950s lakeside cabin built by one of the clients as a teenager with his father. The couple, one a former Navy pilot and both avid sailors, plan to retire there in the summers, while spending the winters aboard their sailboat in the Caribbean. Notions of floating and looping emerged as the conceptual framework for the project. A specific request of the clients was to have an enlarged screen porch, as they spend much time there. The new screen porch is translated as a floating volume that negotiates between the lower sleeping level housed within the existing CMU volume of the former house and the new living level, that floats above.

The existing cabin's simple twenty-four-by-thirty-two-foot masonry shell contrasts with a very lightweight wood-framed roof construction, suggesting the roof's easy removal and replacement with the new program: enlarged living/dining room and home office area. Before the roof's removal, however, a dimensional coincidence between the existing roof construction and wall construction thickness (7.5 inches) is remembered and inspires the new house's strategy of conflating wall-with-roof-with-floor (as in a boat or airplane)—in the form of a single looping plane that houses the new program. This is achieved tectonically through a prefabricated system of eight-inch-deep steel primary roof and floor framing that is coincident with the site-built secondary wood framing system of two-by-eight joists and rafters. Adding to the floating sensation is a ramp that leaves the down-sloping lawn to rise slightly as a gangplank of sorts to the new entrance level. Once inside, one rises slightly again up to the main living level.

Another characteristic of the existing cabin reinterpreted in the new construction is the sense of an outer hard shell and inner soft liner. The new version of this materiality and spatiality exists

in the form of a smooth liner of wood paneling that nests within a
metal-skinned weathering shell. Loop House poses an architecture
in which the spatial and material remembrance of a childhood
event (the act of building the original cabin), the artifact it produced,
and the users' adulthood preoccupation with floating through
space (in planes and boats), are physically and temporally looped
together.

>Project assistant: Timothy Wong

>**top**_>Diagram of spatial loops

>**bottom**/**left**_>Enclosure model

>**bottom**/**right**_>View from dining through living space

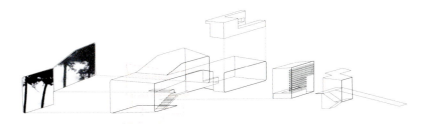

>FLEMINGTON JEWISH COMMUNITY CENTER

>Flemington, New Jersey

>First Prize, International Design Competition

in partnership with Robert Levit as L/IS Levit Iwamoto Scott

>Traditionally, the synagogue is a site of prayer, and its architecture should not become the subject of worship. This ambivalence for the synagogue to be at once a recognizable house of worship and a nonsymbolic place for gathering, is further complicated by the Jewish community center's mixture of heterogeneous programs. Combined with the explicitly religious aspect of the synagogue sanctuary are the social hall, which is secular in its mission, and the school, which is, though certainly a traditional part of religious training, quite separate from the services of the sanctuary. This split between the secular and religious parts of the building is reflected in the underlying twinning of the building's form.

The design works toward constructing such equivocal representations in the relation of its parts. Avoiding an explicitly iconographic program for the synagogue, the scheme's formal strategy holds within a mute exterior envelope the hidden discovery of a glowing sanctuary interior. The orchestration of light emanating from within the ceiling of the synagogue draws upon the tradition that brings forth the un-nameable presence of a higher being while eschewing more explicit evocations of religion. A landscape of luminous glass courtyards and skylights drifts through the space, creating a repetitious pattern that moves through the building's secular and religious figures. This landscape penetrates through the courtyards, countering the closed shape of the building. Daily use requires passage through glass "bridges" that thread these exterior courtyards together in a circulation loop that links all of the programmed space.

>Project team: Olivia Hyde, Je-Uk Kim, Tonino Vicari, Damian Petrescu, Grace Ahn, Sung-Won Lee, Sunil Park

>**left/top**_>Entrance from South Main Street

>**left/center**_>South facade from parking

>**left/bottom**_>View of entrance

>**right**_>Shell/wrapper, roof lights/glass, program voids

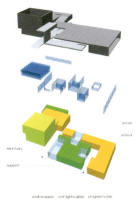

>**top**_>East-facing school elevation

>**center**_>View of sanctuary looking toward ark, with movable wall

opening into social hall at left, multifunctioning ceiling landscape above

>**bottom**_>Luminous volumes

>**top**_>Passage looking through light voids at library/school
>**bottom/left**_>Floor plan
>**bottom/right**_>Roof landscape

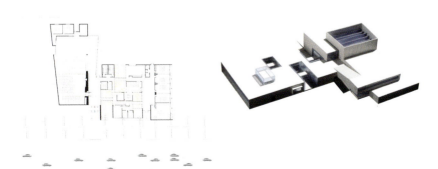

>LIVEWORKSHOPHOUSE

>House: Case Study Cleveland

>Second Prize, Invited Design Competition and Exhibition SPACES Gallery, Cleveland, Ohio

>In response to the reformative nature of the Case Study Cleveland exhibition, our design proposal is simultaneously prototypical, site-specific, and adaptable in nature. The project proceeds along three main conceptual trajectories. The first proposition is that a house design for a compact lot in an urban area that is being re densified should consider the space it makes urbanistically as equally important to the space it contains within. The second engages the particular live-work implications of the given program brief, with both its semipublic element of a graphic designer's studio and its expansion on the typical garage workshop for the restoration of collector cars, through tactics of the formal diagram. The third trajectory involves reassessing attitudes toward building technology and economy of means put forth in John Entenza's Los Angeles Case Study House program.

LiveWorkShopHouse's configurational logic begins with a solid urban block containing the entire house's program, out of which two voids are subtracted that together form a third space—a revisiting of the double-negative concept. The sky void is generated by subtracting the upper southern corner of the house block, letting light and air reach a large extent of the program while also providing an elevated artificial ground plane with a garden and deck. Subtracting the lower northern corner of the house block creates the ground void. It overlaps with the sky void at the house's center, responds to entry on Fifth Street, and allows the living/dining space to extend into a protected courtyard.

The given program's hybrid nature further elaborates the specifics of the double negative configuration in terms of particular spatial orientations and interrelationships developed around the central exterior space. Complementing the house's hybrid program, the scheme deploys a hybrid structure—combining steel with off-the-shelf lightweight prefabricated structure and enclosure systems. As such, the making of spaces, the accommodation of program, the tactility and effects of material are supported by, rather than inscribed within, the system of structure.

In aiming for a reflexive, heterogeneous building system, the design also presumes a flexible menu of finish materials as customizable wrappers and liners. The proposed final design is but one demonstration of a number of possible permutations. This new vision of the affordable, adaptable Case Study House assumes an open-ended, bottom-up attitude that aims more for the transformative whole than the clear articulation of parts. Through such tactics there is an attempt to offer a more pragmatic, performative, and improvisational architecture, one that deploys a spatial paradigm that is clearly prototypical but that also welcomes user input and allows individuality.

>Project team: Nicole Milliff, Grace Ahn, Damien Petrescu, Yongkeun Yoon, Paul Bae, Tonino Vicari, Paul Dragescu, Alec Ng

>**left**_>Initial configurational studies using common prefabricated module sizes

>**center**_>Spatial program diagram integrated with double negative

>**right**_>Stacking of constructional modules

>**top**_>View from road

>**left**_>Plans

>**right/top**_>View from terrace toward alley

>**right/bottom**_>View of living space

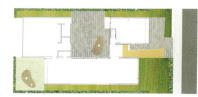

>**top**_>Three variants—thin, medium, wide

>**bottom**_>View at entry

>L.E.FT

>The theme "Material Process" was approached using a tabulation of architectural ingredients that inform the design "process," and become its starting "materials." Along the way, items can beadded, transformed, detailed, renamed, or deleted. It is a barometer for the overall conceptual development of the designs and a uniform tie between diverse projects, each catering for one or more of these items.

"Digestive"_explores the relationship between architecture and consumption, giving precedence to behavioral quantity over spatial quality (e.g. the alcohol in %Bar).

"Catalogue"_parallels the architectural design process to shopping. Architectural history, products, and graphic standards become its inventory (e.g. Home Sweet's Home's summer collection, One Door House's revolving door).

"Finishes"_defines program in its assigned physicality (e.g. the finishes of One Door House).

"Talk"_understands architecture as a form of representation. It identifies the different texts through which architecture can be circulated between architects, with clients, and for the public in general (e.g. concept texts).

"Saturated Aesthetics"_acknowledges the prescribed formal ingredient in the design project (everywhere).

>ONE DOOR HOUSE

>The design begins with a generic condition of the revolving door, interpreting its inherent spatiality, its in-door potential. As a prepolitical *objet trouve* the door is imbued with cultural import, marked by a reading of Lebanese expressions, spatial in nature, yet linguistically paradoxical.

>from inside to inside

A person acts from inside to inside when he is connected to a circle
from within making use of contacts to establish his goals.

>from outside to outside

A person acts from outside to outside when he does not make use of
his contacts, he works from without.

>from here to here

A bargaining tool used to get a better deal in commercial transactions.

Assuming the revolving door is a Duchampian door taken to the power two, it generates a space flattened to minimum connectivity. Zapping occurs between two external quarters, parking and pool (from outside to outside), and two internal ones, living and service (from inside to inside). It produces a collapse between normative domestic notions of front yard and backyard, and front room and back room.

The house is formed by a three-dimensional representation of both inside/inside and outside/outside conditions: Through internal stairs, ground-floor divisions dissolve in the second-floor hallway, which generates a wrapping space; this time inflated to maximum connectivity into a hall, a bourgeois cell.

In parallel, from the parking area one can use a lift to go up to the roof park and from there through an inverted slide into the pool, compressing into the domestic scale the Lebanese urban myth of same-day travel between ski and swimming resorts.

>**top**_>Exit-Exit collage: from outside to outside

>**center**_>Floor plans: ground floor, first floor, roof plan

>**center/right**_>Model photo

>**bottom**_>Rotating elevation, second floor: maximum connectivity

>"Almost space" is a weak space, to be defined in an instanta-
neous collage of architect/client, differing aesthetic judgments and
suspending them. It eludes spatial qualities labeled in architects'
discourses. It politicizes the generic, running the risk of generalizing
the political.

It is incomplete, to be continued...

>**below**_>Rotating perspectives

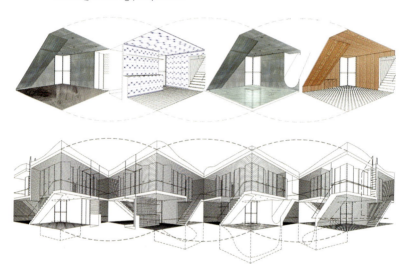

>**top**_>Map of flattened house

>**bottom**_>Map of flattened

neighborhood

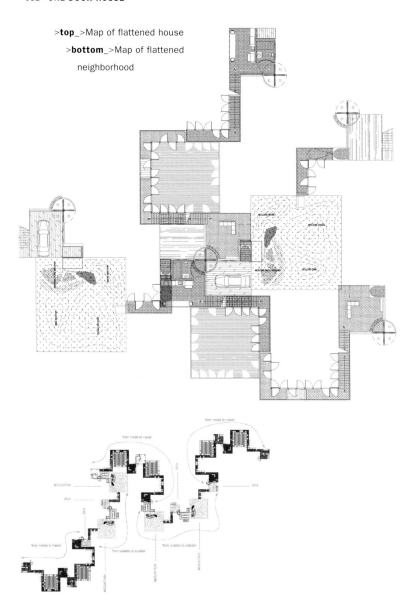

>HOME SWEET'S HOME

>Addition to a house in New Jersey

>Revisiting standardization Home Sweet's Home (HSH) interprets the house as a cross section through Sweet's catalogs—into an off-the-shelf collection of differences rather than repetitions of the same. HSH is the intersection of the architect's ego with the client's wishes—aesthetics with economy, creativity with feasibility, new with familiar; it is a deluxe ordinary.

>**below**_>Exploded axonometry—Sweet's Catalogs

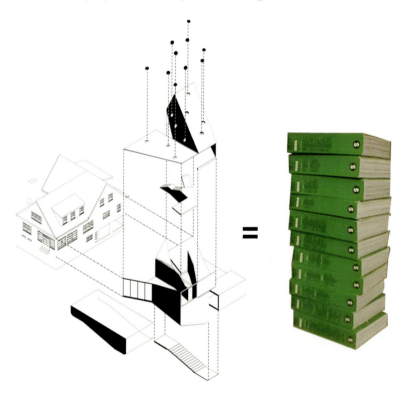

>CATALOGUE
>Summer Collection 2001

>Catalogue is our first attempt in dealing with "architecture *trouvée*" as a design strategy. In the Summer Collection 2001 architectural moments (qualities) are collected from different existing modern resort houses. These moments are then packaged and itemized in an attempt to circulate the designs that are generated within elitist circles. The client can make his or her own house by choosing the moments that he or she desires. The architect's role is to put together the different parts, collapsing the generic with the designed.

>**below**_>Summer Collection 2001 and model photo

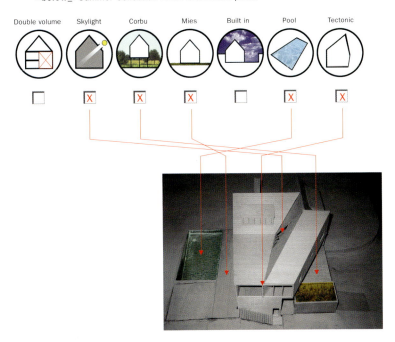

Double volume Skylight Corbu Mies Built in Pool Tectonic

>(Un)feasibility Study tries to represent the aesthetics of the house quantitatively by mapping its materials' value as a spatial means of tracking budget. With the (un)feasibility studies, Value Engineering becomes a design tool.

>**top**_>Spend more

>**bottom**_>Spend less

>Before/After (B/A) tactic tries to escape the dialectic approach of old/new. With B/A there is no need to contrast or otherwise merge. B/A defines a strategy of insertion into the existing condition. Small operations of alterations result in big transformations of the existing architecture. B/A is effectively a representation technique that tries to portray to the client through collage, referencing Catalogue Summer Collection 2001, the available spatial potentials in the existing house with additions and subtractions.

>**top_**>Before/After

>**center/top_**>Before/After collage, sleeping

>**center/bottom_**>Before/After collage, living

>**bottom_**>Before/After collage front yard/backyard

>Entailing a formal disengagement from the author of the design (as opposed to the disinterested viewer), *Form Making* appropriates the client's preconceptions of the form of his or her house as a starting point. After conceptually interpreting the form and defining the final massing, the client's wishes are introduced into the form explicitly. The house witnesses the client's imprints.

The earned privacy of the client's eighteen-year-old daughter transformed the family structure. The new extrusion divides the backyard, providing a dual role of the house.

The existing house is layered horizontally: backyard/parking, front yard/living, and views/sleeping. The addition, as a back extrusion across the full width of the existing facade, creates a double loop of sleeping/living/parking for the family that centers itself in the kitchen. Ease of access to the kitchen, parental control, and the daughter's privacy are coupled with an attempt to deal with family politics.

The husband's study and the wife's kitchen share a two-way visual control through a central gap in the new addition that collapses front yard and backyard, thus allowing a minimum walking distance from parking to kitchen, creating a new circulation zone for the house.

>**below**_>Diagrams

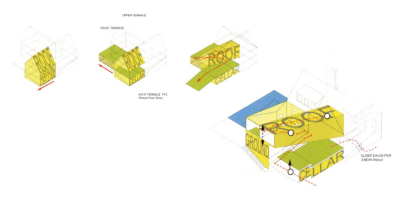

>**top**_>Plan

>**center**_>Section

>**bottom**_>Model

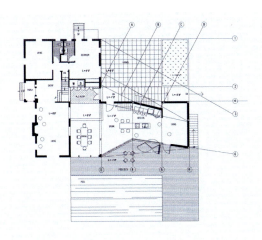

>SURROUND DATAHOME

>Assuming suburbia resolved, let's scramble it.

>The suburban ideal finds its utmost representation in zoning as a programmatic model.

Isolation of living (domesticity) from working, shopping, and recreation becomes its predicament. Paradoxically, the proliferation of such amenities is based on their ability to simulate, xeroxing the same domestic environment they try to substitute.

To this domestication of the corporate, the proximity of datahome to its surroundings offers an opportunity to reverse this process by franchising the domestic.

Datahome becomes formally manifest in a subtractive combination with its surrogates. Next to a hotel, Datahome subtracts its bedrooms, next to a gym, its bathroom. Datahome's degree zero is its self-demise, a total parasite living on its surroundings. This is the condition of the homeless jetsetters, or, in culture jamming terms, of squatters.

>**below**_>Rubikfact: forty-three quintillion is forty-three million million million. There are only about thirty million seconds in a year. You would need over a thousand million years, looking at a thousand patterns every second, to see all the combinations possible with Rubik's cube.

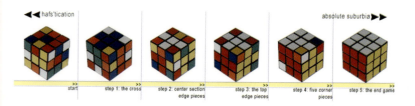

◀◀ hafs'tication   absolute suburbia ▶▶

| >> start | >> step 1: the cross | >> step 2: center section edge pieces | >> step 3: the top edge pieces | >> step 4: five corner pieces | >> step 5: the end game |

>**top/left**_>Absolute suburbia syngraphai

>**top/right**_>Absolute suburbia model

>**bottom**_>Scrambled suburbia model

>Datahome becomes an intersection of collectivities where individuals can maneuver the tools provided by the corporate world. It exists in suspension from the ideal condition it originated from. To reclaim privacy, the upper level reinterprets suburbia as mezzanine. The elevator button swaps between the conditions of urbanity and suburbanity (in this case super urbanity), between publicity and privacy.

>**below_**>Scrambled suburbia plan (drawing not for construction)

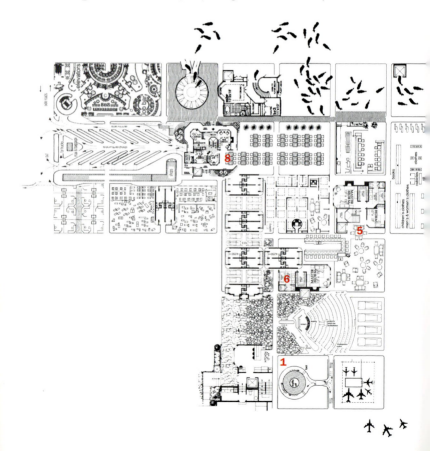

>**top/left**_>**1**_Home minus parking

>**top/right**_>**2**_Home minus TV room: TV turnoff week April 22–28

>**center**_>**3**_Home minus storage: the more you consume, the less you live

>**bottom**_>**4**_Home minus kitchen: come and prepare your own quick
meal at home, thanks

>**top**_>**5**_Home minus living: extended living, please trespass

>**bottom/left**_>**6**_Home minus bedroom: capsule hotel

>**bottom/center**_>**7**_Home minus bathroom

>**bottom/right**_>**8**_Home minus dining

>BED, BATH, AND BEYOND

>A prototype for a boutique hotel room

>In collaboration with Lewis-Tsurumaki-Lewis

>Since hotel time is divided equally between bedroom and bathroom, the design proposes that half the room be a continuous tiled surface that, when filled with water, serves as a large bathing pool; the other half becomes a continuous bed surface made of resilient foam and surface-mounted sheets with Velcro stays.

The variable softness of the bed and the variable water level of the bath/pool allow each room to perform multiple functions in a minimum of space—from foot washing to full body immersion, from lounging to sleeping. A grid of shower sprays on the bathroom ceiling is mirrored by pin spotlights above the bed; one can shower or read/work in any portion of the bed or bathroom.

At the line of division a flat-screen television suspended from a ceiling-mounted track can be rotated to face either side of the room. This monitor provides access to the Internet and cable television, electronic interaction with the hotel concierge, and billing information. The room's horizontal work/utility surfaces are a continuous stainless steel element. The remainder of the equipment and storage is consolidated in the wall adjacent to the corridor.

>**below**_>The design began by tracing the spectrum of the different types of accommodation, by trying to collapse the generic (capsule hotel) with the customized (a designed house).

laundromat   capsule hotel   luxury hotel room   house

100%   QUANTITY*   0%

0%   QUALITY*   100%

>**top+bottom**_>Bed and bath perspectives

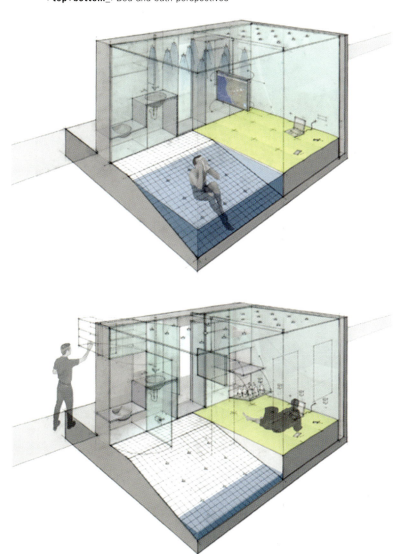

>The program in %Bar is reduced to two activities: drinking and urinating.

A BAC line (estimating Blood Alcohol Content) connects the bar's counter to the toilet door, and becomes the threshold between drunkenness and soberness. Along this line the percentages of alcohol in the blood (BAC levels) are annotated. It becomes the fold of the ground plane. With a 5% slope, starting from the entry point (0.01% BAC), it gives a one-foot height advantage and hence a better visibility to the sober person coming into the space looking for his or her buddies. It also gives the drunk person walking along it (instantaneous spectacle) a clear path to the toilet to throw up, and back to the bar to refill. The glowing surrounding walls render the crowd as a silhouette. Smaller spaces are wrapped with latex curtains allowing an explicit conceal/reveal relationship with the main central space.

>**left_**>BAC spatial interpretation
>**right_**>Silhouette, path and latex

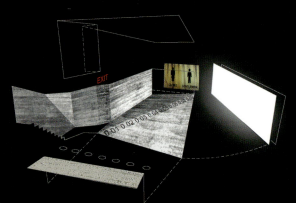

>**top**_>Plan and section

>**bottom**_>Exploded axonometry

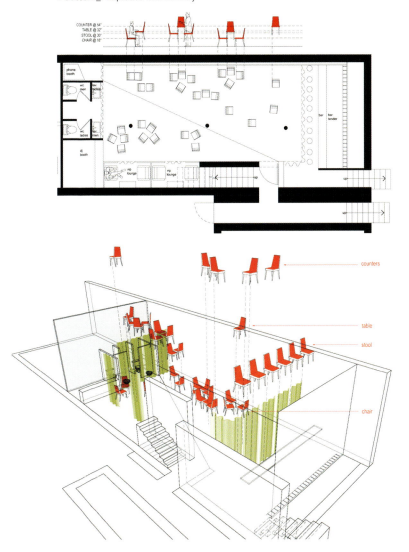

>YOUNG ARCHITECTS FORUM 2002

>New York City

>The installation starts from the available materials of the gallery: a floor with three sockets. Each socket spreads into five light fixtures made of bent steel with "down-up" curtains that hold the project information and a fluorescent bulb. This composition reconstructs the floor as an inverted ceiling.

>**below**_>Photos of Installation, May 2002

>CONFESSIONAL POLITICS

>The Lebanese secular and religious societies are often seen in mutually exclusive stances. There is a conflict of interest at the origin of a separation (zonal segregation) between the architectural manifestations of these societies (clubs versus church/mosque). The purpose of this study is to show the level of this architectural manifestation and to demonstrate that a common infrastructure exists in this dialectic.

The infrastructure of these two typologies (religious/secular) is seen here as raw material that, once adopted spatially, gains an interpretive aspect specific to each:

-wine consumption in both

-music versus call for prayer (insulated/extroverted)

-fog machine versus incense

-artificial light versus natural light

This raw material is symbolically as well as quantitatively differentiated in each space. The percentage of consumption becomes a measure that dictates the quality of both.

>**below**_>Installation infrastructure

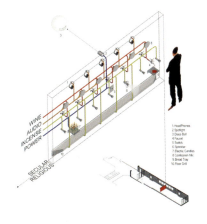

>LEFTISHTALKONDISCOURSE

>By dissipating architectural talk to a more general audience, away from the closed circles of the discipline, architectural representation in that public realm becomes of interest. In its attempt to flirt with a lost autonomy (assuming it once existed), the relation of architecture to commercialization has always been one of skepticism. In varying degrees the disengagement of critical architectural discourse from commercial forms of dissemination and the noncritical embrace of the popular taste at the other end, lead to a missed opportunity in using the content of the first with the methods of the latter to the benefit of the discipline.

Two magazines at the two extremes of architecture's representation, *Assemblage* and *Architectural Digest,* epitomize this dilemma. The assumption here is that in order to keep a critical edge toward architecture's production, one must refrain from indulging in the actual commercial processes of this production. Conversely, the concern becomes adopting a subordinate attitude toward a more popular aesthetic and formal thought. Profiting from a widespread audience that naturalizes it, this thought is still a constructed one, and hence apt to intellectual scrutiny.

Some magazines that try to situate themselves in the middle of the spectrum (e.g. *Architectural Record*) fail to stretch the envelope beyond the professional space.

leftishtalkondiscourse mapped the commercial content of *Architectural Record* over a period of ten years, and the public interest for the Architectural League lectures (through an opinion poll taken after lectures).

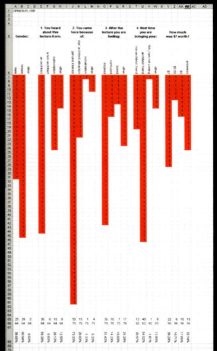

>MESH

>While so much of digitization in architecture has focused on flashy renderings and non-orthogonal geometry, what is most interesting is how digital technologies are altering our environment. We have gradually learned to dwell in cyberspace, to see the networked database spaces as extensions of our built world.

Since the founding of my firm four years ago, my work has entailed the integration and crossing over of disciplines. We design both architectural spaces and web sites with a focused objective of forging new relationships between people and their environments in the age of the network.

In the last couple of years, we have begun to use digital tools in the manufacturing and production process. For the fiberglass wall of the Downtown Duplex we emailed our digital drawings to Cleveland for production. Contoured countertops are computer-cut in Massachusetts from digital templates. We have enjoyed a collaborative relationship with Panelite, an innovative manufacturer of composite panels, which has led to new material applications of new materials, using glass/honeycomb panels as unframed office walls, FRP/honeycomb panels as floors and ceilings, polycarbonate/acrylic (Norcore) panels as lightwalls, and casting polycarbonate core in acrylic resin to form curved panels.

On a low-tech level we output computer drawings as full-scale templates. For the Synth installation we built videogame chairs by cutting sections out of Styrofoam from overlaid templates.

Digitization has crossed over into lighting as well. A new generation of LEDs and controllers is changing how we think about lights. Like pixels of a computer display, these lights project millions of colors and intensities. The software enables manipulation of the environment over time, allowing architecture to extend into this fourth dimension. The lights may also be controlled over the Internet.

Much has been written about the flux of digital information through our home and work spaces, but we have only begun to imagine the material imprint of the networked digital media upon our environments. How are we going to receive, project, and respond to them, physically and by projecting our consciousness? We will soon see more clearly the extension of spaces through the network.

>DOWNTOWN DUPLEX

>New York City

>The duplex starts from the concept of a loft as a microcosmic urban space, an oversized setting for activities and events. By creating loosely connected zones with varied environments, the home becomes a dynamic setting for exploration and concentration.

An area of the second floor, between the parents' and children's wings, is removed. A green fiberglass wall runs along the length of the two-story space containing the loft infrastructure (ducts, electrical conduit, plumbing, and lighting).

Small LCD screens throughout the space, embedded in walls, furniture, and cabinetry, provide access to the Home Operating System, a web-based home control and communication system. This system is not only internal, but it connects the micro-urban space of the loft out to the electronic urban space of the web. This exterior-viewless home becomes at once an inward-focused sanctuary and an active site for mediated connection to the outside world.

>Project team: Eric Liftin, Thomas Kearns

>**below**_>Model of fiberglass wall, lower level

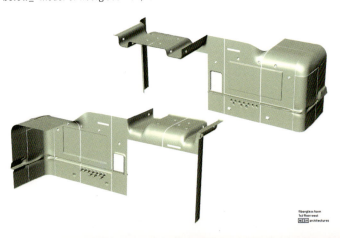

fiberglass foam
1st floor west
MESH architectures

>**top**_>Section, construction drawing

>**center**_>Sectional rendering

>**bottom**_>Diagram of intranetwork

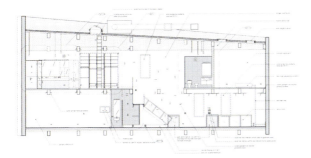

>**top/left**_>Stair and LED light wall

>**top/right**_>Pipe lights

>**bottom/left**_>Fiberglass envelope contains plumbing, CCTV, a/c, and pipe lights. Work niche in back.

>**bottom/right**_>Bathroom, stair, closet

>**top/left+center**_>Rendering and photo of upper-level bridge

>**top/right**_>View over garden to bedroom lounge

>**center**_>Bridge over old beams

>**bottom**_>View through garden to eating area

>MERCER STREET "DENSITY" LOFT

>New York City

>This loft renovation provides a new downtown environment for a
father and his grown children. There are three major elements
inserted into the voluminous space: the children's rooms, the kitchen,
and the master suite, a multi-story, dense, layered sequence
of rooms.

We maximized the open, unprogrammed space, leaving it loose and
"loftlike" for family living, then delineated the bedroom, bath, and
storage volumes with a three-dimensional steel grid, into which we
inserted wood cabinets, glass floor panels and translucent plastic
panels and shelves, to create a dense, controlled environment. The
children's block counterbalances the owner's private quarters. The
steel grid is activated throughout by computer-controlled LED lights,
which are programmed to run a number of "shows" and can respond
to signals from the Internet. Glass catwalks enable varied explorations
of the space, creating the effect of a hovering partial presence, an
in-between space mediating the suite and the open space.

>Project team: Eric Liftin, George Roushakes, Greg Merryweather

>**below**_>Interior rendering

>**top**_>Main space (under construction)

>**bottom/left**_>Steel/acrylic wall model

>**bottom/right**_>Catwalk detail

>**top**_>Details: steel frame, Panelite, acrylic, glass, wood panels
>**top/right**_>Powder room with resin-embedded gravel floor
>**bottom/left**_>Cantilevered steel/acrylic stair, digital lighting
>**bottom/right**_>Digital lighting sequencing program

>GREENWICH STREET LOFT

>New York City

>A familiar story: an old warehouse space becomes a home. A media wall slices through on the diagonal, connecting front to back while opening the central space to western views. Paneled in fiberglass-reinforced plastic, the wall is full of lighting, sound, and network cable. An opening in the wall allows an inhabitable cube on casters to emerge or act as a projection device.

Project team: Eric Liftin, Sara Moss, Galia Solomonoff

>**top/left_**>Layout showing lightwall and cube
>**top/right_**>Lightwall bright
>**bottom/left_**>Lightwall bright, cube pushed in
>**bottom/right_**>Open bathroom

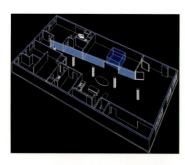 

>**below**_>Main space, lightwall dim, cube projecting

>OSCAR BOND SALON

>New York City

>In association with Jordan Parnass/Digital Architecture

>The design for the Oscar Bond Salon presents a new concept, expanding the term *salon* to propose a space for complex interaction among patrons, stylists, and, via the Internet, anybody who wants to participate. The salon is networked for Internet and video signals.

The web site space is continuous with the salon. Through web cams and custom server software, the site enables communication between the salon and the rest of the web.

An extended aluminum runway brings visitors down into the space. Contrary to the design of most salons, the waiting corral is the nexus of the space, a raised platform with net-connected computers and a video monitor.

>Project team: Eric Liftin, Jordan Parnass, Soyeon Kim, Sara Moss

>**left**_>Salon web site

>**right**_>Reception

>**top/left**_>Entry stair

>**top/center**_>View from entry

>**top/right**_>Hair drying station

>**bottom**_>Central waiting corral

>RANDOM ACCESS MEMORY

>An experiment in collective recollection

>http://randomaccessmemory.org

>This is a backup archive for personal memories, for recollections important or trivial. Contribute your memories, and they are stored by date and browsable by date, subject, or name. RAM is a demonstration of what happens when personal information is compiled into a database that is accessible on a pseudonymous basis. Thus it performs two roles simultaneously: private and public. It stores personal information for the user, and it aggregates and indexes this information to amuse and enlighten all visitors. As more people use the system, patterns emerge and we can observe what kinds of memories characterize certain years.

You must enter a date, a person, or a subject to view the memories. From any set of displayed memories, there are hyperlinks to the people and dates in the list. As with human memory, you cannot simply dump the database: cues at the surface lead to associations, which generate further associations.

>Project team: Eric Liftin, John Donovan

>9-11-01 RANDOM ACCESS MEMORIAL

>http://randomaccessmemorial.org

>This version of Random Access Memory was launched in the week following the September 11 terrorist attacks as a dedicated site to record the memories of people who lived through the events. As with RAM, the memories are kept for the user as a journal and are also accessible to visitors to the site. Because visitors can enter a victim's name in connection with a memory, the site can also be used to create collective memorials to victims.

>RANDOM ACCESS MEMORIAL/"TIME TO CONSIDER" POSTER

>2/02 New York City

>This poster is an attempt to document a complex, traumatic event by recalling reactions in the streets and evoking memories. It was published as part of a project, "Time To Consider," by Creative Time, Worldstudio, and the Van Alen Institute.

The images are video stills from downtown Manhattan taken on September 11 and September 12 and filtered to remove detail. The superimposed bubbles ask viewers to contribute memories. Passers-

by who encounter the poster may reconnect with their experiences of September 11 and spontaneously write recollections in the bubbles. The URL on the poster links to more memories at www.randomaccessmemorial.org.

In an urban context the connection between the street, experience, and memory is critical. People are exposed to the limits of experience in public space in the presence of strangers, but bonded by the communal environment of the city.

>MILESTONE VENTURE PARTNERS
>New York City

>An Internet venture fund wanted to transform a tight, low-slung slice of midtown space into a suitable environment for high-tech finance. Three loosely affiliated companies share the space. The problem was to transform a conventional office layout into a layered, luminous space with a sense of depth.

MESH divided the private offices with glowing Lumasite (fiberglass reinforced acrylic) clad walls packed with data, power, and television cable. The walls provide both physical storage and electr(on)ic connectivity, and continue into the corridor as ambient light boxes.

Perpendicular to these displays, the walls dividing the offices and corridor are of structural glass/honeycomb core–composite panels (an experimental material). The panels provide a degree of transparency that shifts in relation to the viewing angle and distance.

>Project team: Eric Liftin, Thomas Kearns, Peter Kopitz, David Fratianne

>**left**_>Reception
>**right**_>Corridor with glass/honeycomb walls and doors

>**top**_>Reception

>**bottom**_>Material details

>SYNTH

>New York City

>http://www.whitecolumns.org/synth

>This exhibition at White Columns, a New York gallery space, explored the dissolving boundaries between the synthetic and organic through the creation of immersive installations within a large-scale inflatable structure. Each synthetic work feels active and seemingly alive, but in reality has been created by computer technology.

MESH collaborated with organizer Leo Villareal on the exhibition design as well as on designing environments to house interactive, projected installations. Two synth chairs represent an inversion of a chaise longue, supporting the players of a networked video game in a forward-leaning, active position, in contrast to the slouch familiar to sofa-based gamers.

>Project team: Eric Liftin, Thomas Kearns, Peter Kopitz

>**left**_>Marathon room model

>**right**_>Installation models

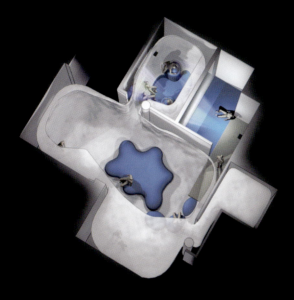

>TKTS COMPETITION

>New York City

>Competition sponsored by the Van Alen Institute and
Theatre Development Fund

>The tkts pavilion does not just sell tickets. It becomes a device
to redirect energy of Times Square out over the Internet. This project
would establish tkts2k.net as a direct link to the spectacle of
Times Square and the world of Broadway shows by creating a network, connecting Times Square, Broadway theaters, and people
worldwide. The result is a grand twenty-four-hour global theater projecting the life of Times Square.

The translucent boxes are constructed of self-supporting sand-
wich panels, and the electronic mantle is fiberglass. The mantle
opens during selling hours to expose ticket windows and closes at
other times to expose only the tkts2k.net interface.

>Project team: Eric Liftin, Thomas Kearns

>**left**_>Section view

>**top**_>Concept diagram

>**center**_>Web site mockup and plan

>**bottom**_>Site view

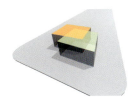

>LEAF LIGHT

This light fixture was designed in three-dimensional software around a digital LED lamp and changes colors over time. A stereo lithography process generated the leaf object directly from the three-dimensional file.

>Project team: Eric Liftin

>MESH SITE

>http://www.mesh-arc.com

>An exploration of a conceptual two-dimensional/three-dimensional space. Arranged as a virtual stack of cards, which can be shuffled to create various configurations, the space was built in Flash and uses the program's native animation vocabulary.

Each card is a field for actions: images, animation, text. The cards have holes in them that lead through to the next card in the stack. A tunneling animation effects the transition. The linear navigation is counterposed by the stack navigator, which enables visitors to select a particular card to visit. By assigning each project a card, the portfolio of work can be endlessly sorted by date, project type, or anything else. The "graffiti box" provides a place for visitors to leave their commentary.

>MOTT STREET LOFT

>New York City

>The New York loft presents a formidable design exercise. How many ways can a loft be programmed for discrete activities without being turned into an apartment? For these two writers MESH divided the rectangular space laterally into zones: public spaces in the front and private spaces (bedroom and studies) in the back. The zone in between, however, is convertible. It is a library whose shelves can open completely or close to become a den, thus modulating the entire scheme. The bathroom is a Panelite cubic volume, hovering and glowing behind the library.

>Project team: Eric Liftin, Thomas Kearns

>**left**_>Convertible library with mobile shelves and chaise longue

>**right**_>View of space, showing convertible library

>**bottom**_>Panelite bath from main space

>TIMES CAPSULE

>Launched 12/99

>In collaboration with Benjamin Strouse, Michael Rock of 2x4,
John Stewart, David Reinfurt

>The New York Times held an invited competition to design a millen-
nial time capsule. This proposal uses the Internet (the only proposal
to do so) to create a worldwide, material time capsule network
that would survive the electronic network. The web site would help
participants organize their own, physical time capsules and link
them into a physical network. After the web fades into its successors,
the buried capsules remain, connected through information.

>**below**_>Diagram of Times Capsule network

TimesCapsule.net

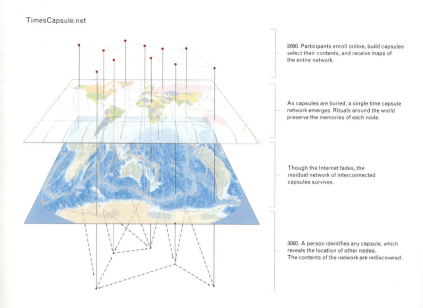

2000. Participants enroll online, build capsules
select their contents, and receive maps of
the entire network.

As capsules are buried, a single time capsule
network emerges. Rituals around the world
preserve the memories of each node.

Though the Internet fades, the
residual network of interconnected
capsules survives.

3000. A person identifies any capsule, which
reveals the location of other nodes.
The contents of the network are rediscovered.

>IOMESH LIBRARY

> Launched 01/99

>This is an experiment in an integrated online and physical library, based on the principle that a library for the information age is shaped more by the people who use it than by its collection. Patrons leave digital footprints that create links among the contents of the library. Entry in Acadia's (http://www.acadia.org/) design competition.

>**left**_>Sample entry from Iomesh Library

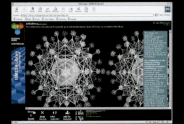

>DELLA VALLE + BERNHEIMER DESIGN

>*Anything will give up its secrets if you love it enough.*
—George Washington Carver, inventor

>*Everything should be made as simple as possible, but not one bit simpler.*
—Albert Einstein, inventor

>*The art of progress is to preserve order amid change and to preserve change amid order.*
—Alfred North Whitehead, mathematician

>A little honesty to start: We (architects, that is) do not reinvent materials. We never have. What happens is this: We fiddle with shapes, argue about program, reason with our clients, and then, ultimately, get a little lucky and locate the right moment to reuse the inventions of others. In turn, we get credit for rethinking the idea of how to build. It is a nice and not entirely undeserved result, actually, this perception of architecture as some sort of conduit for innovation. Instead of being perceived as a community of hangers-on, we are often seen as the bringers of cities, as Edisonian inventors of community and art, or Salkian healers of broken environments.

But, we are, in reality, just shrewdly and creatively implementing connective thoughts and happy accidents, like seeing a picture of an airplane at the same time we are exploring domestic architecture and thinking, "how do I make this a home," or seeing an automobile crash impact test on a televised public service announcement at the same time we are designing a loft and thinking "can I use that material they use in those tests as a wall?"

Our small, New York–based practice is founded on recognizing moments of simultaneity and on breeding unexpectedness through the innovative use of the familiar and the available. We have used laser fabrication and modern steel-rolling technology to create a flexible artist's loft because gray was a desirable color for our artist client and such technology was malleable, inexpensive, highly tolerant, and allowed us to manage out-of-state construction remotely. We have used laser-etched steel in an elementary school library on Staten Island because it will remind kids of subway cars and because, as in the artist's loft, we know that it will end up being fabricated perfectly. We used a massive library of books as a wall in a house because books are familiar, dramatic, enlightening, sometimes funny, and make an amazing texture out of paper, color, and shadows. We also wanted to use (literally) miles and miles of wire to wrap a client's bedroom because it would privatize this area of the loft, let a provocative bit of light through, and look amazingly strange. Unfortunately, our client disagreed.

Our portfolio of work, in which different projects rarely share materials, has evolved while playing a waiting game. We insist on looking, listening, and researching both form and material in an effort to locate those moments when we can get our clients (and ourselves!) to realize that there actually is a kind of invention in familiarity, and that there is inspiration in waiting for the right time to mix things up. Our reward is the mantle of inventor, the satisfaction of knowing that we can make new things out of those that are both intimately and vaguely familiar.

>PLAZA RENOVATION

>450 Golden Gate Avenue, San Francisco, California

>The design for the Federal Plaza, won via an open international design competition, answered a demand in the competition brief to address local issues of habitability, wind control, light, and, as termed in the brief, the "poetics of security."

Working at an urban scale (the site is 125 feet wide by 400 feet long), it was imperative to invent a tool that was able to reduce a large-scale architectural action into an intimate setting. The tool we utilized was a single line: an enormous tilted plane that slopes from the low end of the site to the front of the building at the center of the plaza. This tilt continues to the opposite end of the site, it rises a total of ten feet above the existing grade, creating an increasingly secure barrier between street and plaza. Because of the length of the site, all code issues become a nonfactor: the slope ascends so slowly that landings and handrails become unnecessary. In this way, the stigma of an accessible entry is avoided. All traffic utilizes the same path of travel. Moreover, this single line becomes a generating tool for reducing the scale of such an immense site. Additional intermittent folds and tilts are used as locations for light fixtures, seating areas, and tree and flower planters.

>**below**_>Golden Gate Avenue, composite elevation

>**below**_>Conceptual sketch

>**top/left**_>West wall

>**top/right**_>Golden Gate Avenue center ramp

>**bottom**_>West end

>**top**_>Plan

>**left/center**_>Section at elevated plaza

>**left/bottom**_>Golden Gate Avenue center ramp

>**bottom/right**_>Aerial view

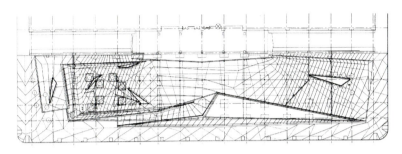

>ETEKT LIBRARY HOUSE

>Conceptual Project

>This house, a retreat for a reader, is a simple and minimal container. A concrete and glass box, the house contains bookshelves capable of storing over five thousand volumes. It is our intention that any owner of this house will use it in virtual solitude, and that being surrounded by books will relax, inspire, and educate.

To this end, a compact book list is enclosed as part of the specifications for the project. The contractor selected to build this house is required (as said list is part of the construction specifications) to supply the new owner with all books on the attached list. This list consists of approximately six hundred books, in print and readily available, which vary in subject matter and theme. The books were selected with diversity in mind—they cover art, politics, history, music, Eastern and Western philosophy, poetry, fiction, dance, architecture, etc. This list is seen as either the start of a new collection or a supplement to an existing collection.

Materially, the house is made of board-formed concrete. A volume, privileged to one side of the house, contains two bathrooms, a dressing and closet area, and a kitchen. The remainder of the house, bordered on three sides by glass, is the library, with the mass of glass bookshelves along the longitudinal perimeter wall. A Murphy Bed is concealed in the long concrete wall and protracts when necessary. Additional privacy can be attained through concealed shades, which retract into the ceiling when openness is desired. Thus, the house can be subdivided into three rooms, giving privacy in the event that guests are invited.

This house was presented as part of a catalog of homes for sale on the ETEKT website (www.etekt.com), a web-commerce company devoted to the sale of contemporary stock house plans.

>*The library is unlimited but periodic. If an eternal traveler should journey in any direction, he would find after untold centuries that the same volumes are repeated in the same disorder—which, repeated, becomes order: the Order. My solitude is cheered by that elegant hope.*

   —Jorge Luis Borges, *The Library of Babylon*, 1941.

>**top_**>Conceptual sketch
>>**center_**>Main elevation with bookshelves
>>>**bottom/left_**>View of main space
>>>>**bottom/right_**>House plan

>HARVEY MILK PLAZA

>2000 San Francisco Prize Competition Entry

>RESURFACE—

>*v. tr.*

To cover with a new surface: *resurfacing a road; resurfaced the floor.*

>*v. intr.*

To come to the surface again; reappear: *The story has resurfaced.*

>This project is the intersection of two surfaces, one existing and one new, as well as a series of lighting sources that will color and shade these redefined surfaces.

The existing streetscape within the defined competition zone will be resurfaced with white stone, and all surrounding buildings within this zone will be painted white, creating a neutral backdrop for a vibrant community of people and activity. In daylight this surface will receive bright sun, shadows, and natural reflections. At night pendant lights hanging from existing tension wires, glowing benches, curb lights, and other artificial sources will serve to illuminate the street and its surroundings, kaleidoscopically altering this new physical landscape.

>*...We don't need another concrete jungle that dies the moment you turn off the lights in the evening.*

>*To sit on the front steps—whether it's a veranda in a small town or a concrete stoop in a big city—is infinitely more important than to huddle on the living room lounger and watch a make-believe world in not-quite living color.*
—Harvey Milk

>**below**_>Conceptual sketch

milk plaza 5.17.00

>**top**_>Daytime plan

>**bottom**_>Night plan

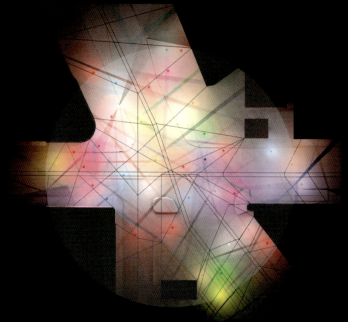

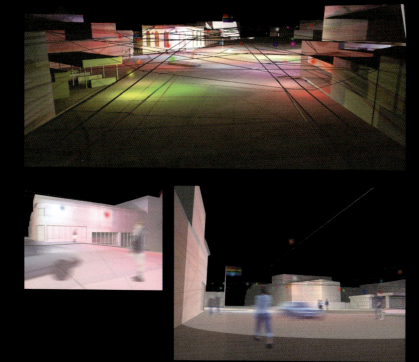

>P.S. 18 LIBRARY

>Staten Island, New York

>There are three encounters at P.S. 18: First, one encounters the box, a gleaming metal object, occupying the space of the hallway and fostering curiosity. It appears as a solid object accessible through two pivoting doors that give a small glimpse of the activity inside through windows at child's height. Second, there is the encounter of a compressed space, filled with information—the book stacks. These are located inside the box. Third, there is the light and colorful laboratory, where one may settle down with information gathered in the book stacks. The interior of the library, bordered on one side by the stainless steel box, contains computers, a reading stage, pinup boards, tables and chairs, and additional storage for teaching materials.

The major materials used in the library at P.S. 18 are stainless steel (for the box), red epoxy (for the floor), clear-finished birch plywood (for the bookshelves), sanded homasote (for the pinup boards), and chalkboard and marker-board facing (for the surfacing of most tables).

>**below**_>Plan

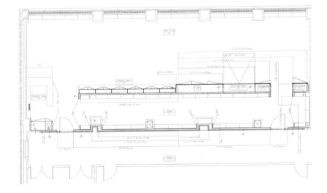

>**top**_>Conceptual sketch
>**bottom**_>Section

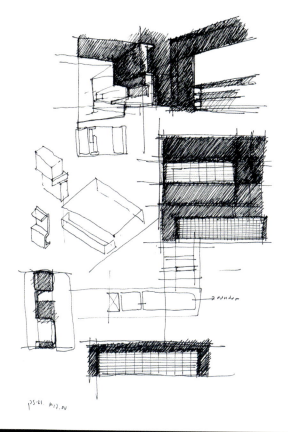

>**top**_>Storytelling area

>**bottom/left**_>Entry

>**bottom/right**_>Door detail

>**top**_>View at main bookshelves

>**bottom**_>Main classroom

>ARTIST'S LOFT

>Boston, Massachusetts

>This loft in Boston was designed for a ceramicist and painter, and her husband, an inventor and computer scientist. The clients demanded three distinct types of spaces: private/domestic, public/studio, and private/studio. Our solution was to strike two lines through the space that bow and flex as programmatic requirements grow or shrink. The northernmost line separates the private area of the loft, containing the master bedroom and the bathrooms. The southernmost line separates the private studio area of the loft, containing a ceramics studio and meditation space. The remaining area of the apartment, between these two long curvilinear walls, houses a kitchen and painting studio, which becomes a display area for the work of the artist when the loft transforms into a gallery at intermittent times during the year for public viewing sessions.

The two walls are fabricated from laser-cut steel. The artist demanded a neutral palette in the apartment, and the steel walls will be a tonally quiet and texturally rich background for her work. These metal panels are punctuated by perforations that are spaces for door pulls and holes for hanging hooks for the artist's work. The laser-cutting technology allowed us to compose the panels with a great deal of freedom and precision—it was an economically efficient and technically accurate process. In order to attain spatial flexibility and efficiency, we designed a wall system that relieved these walls of their commonly inflexible nature: nearly all of the panels pivot as conventional, closet, or pantry doors.

>**top**_>View to kitchen

>**bottom**_>Sketch plan

>**top/left_**>View from kitchen

>**top/right_**>View to meditation space

>**bottom/left_**>Door detail

>**bottom/right_**>Plan

>**below**_>Entry view

>AQUACENTER

>Alborg, Denmark, Swimming Facility Competition

>During the action of swimming, one actively breaks and alters a changing, fluid landscape. This action requires at least two intense commitments: the first to a physical exertion in the interest of exercise, repetitive motion, and energetic release, and the second to an emotional willingness to suspend oneself in a liquid that can envelop, pacify, but also drown. Our project presents to the users of the Aquacenter in Alborg a dual image of dream and fantasy—the vision of people engaging (but not breaking) the surface of water while others puncture and possess that same, transmutable volume.

Our project depends on the visual perception of thickness. From the exterior of the building, the pool appears as a sheer surface, undisturbed by activity, on which participants can walk. However, these people illogically float on a material physically unsuited for any such foot traffic, and the visualization of a vast volume of presumably thick water is subverted by the realization that in places it is actually very thin. Similarly, the underside of the pool appears as a sculptural surface, exposed as a thick architectural tool, honest in its appearance. As such, a diving pool abuts a circuit pool, which abuts a barely submerged walking path that abuts a wading pool. These various pools are available by an infinite number of individually chosen routes—there is no internal hierarchy to the pool arrangement.

On the lower level of the Aquacenter, the underside of the pool acts as a ceiling to the spa and locker rooms—access is gained to the main swimming space by a stair ascending into an area surrounded on all sides by water. Thus, a visitor encounters the "underside of the ocean," and replicates an act of resurfacing, but at a point prior to getting wet. This initial engagement with the physical construct of the Aquacenter concludes with the physical act of swimming and with the strange, fascinating illusion of people walking on water.

>**below**_>Design sketch

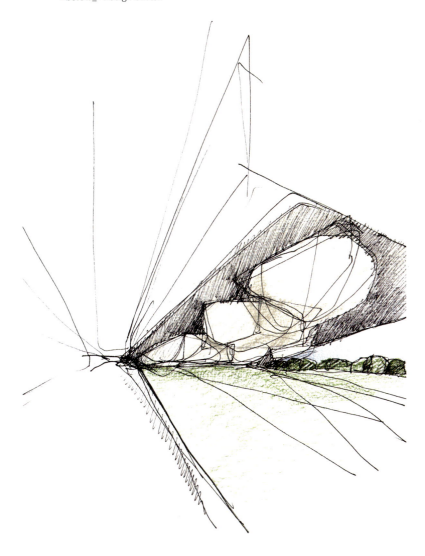

>**top**_>Swimming pool plan

>**center**_>Main building section

>**bottom**__>Entry elevation

>**below**_>Exploded axonometric

>**top**_>Circuit pool rendering

>**bottom**_>Exterior deck rendering

>SOHO LOFT

>New York City

>Thin gauge wire wrapping a metal structure defines a bedroom and bathroom suite in a large, open loft space.

>OFFICE FOR WINE IMPORTER

>New York City

Burgundy liquid inside a glass frame creates a murky barrier between a conference room and a showroom, presenting the illusion of people immersed in wine.

>J. MEEJIN YOON

>emBODIED TECTONICS

>"Tectonics" has become a mutable and unstable term. Truth in materials or in methods of construction is no longer (and arguably never was) an absolute concept. While the design of materials is not new, the recent evolution of mutant materials and fabrication technologies has created a material culture pregnant with possibilities. Plastics can be endowed with the properties of glass, wood made to appear like fabric, and foams given the power of memory. Materials and their methods are multiplying while our inherited notions of architectural material significance and signification are increasingly challenged.

Material instability coupled with emergent digital design technologies are transforming the role of the architect and the boundaries of the discipline. The integration of computer-aided design and manufacturing (CAD/CAM) has not only created new potentials for design and fabrication but has altered the way in which many architects engage the design process. Parametric modeling and computer numerically controlled (CNC) machines allow for increasing flexibility and expediency during the design and fabrication process. While these technologies create new possibilities in design and fabrication, they also privilege specific modes of working and set new limits, requiring architects to be critical within a process that seamlessly moves from input to output.

The following work examines the mutability of materials and their technologies with respect to the body and its material envelopes: skin, clothing, and architecture. The skin is not only the body's most immediate envelope but also its largest organ and most sophisticated container. Textile fabrics (clothing), building fabrics (architecture), and urban fabrics (cities) become potential second, third, and fourth skins. The following projects blur the distinctions between these categories, operating simultaneously on the body and its multiple claddings as a spatial and material inquiry to inscribe, contain, and extend the body in space. The Acu-puncture Vest negotiates between the flatness of the acupressure map and the contours of the body to mold and map its pressure points onto the body. The Defensible Dress clothes the body in an electronically enabled garment that reinscribes notions of personal space. The Interactive Pleated Wall interacts with viewing bodies, responding to their presence through digitally interactive components. The Between Bodies and Walls studio explores the mutability of material concepts as a means to engage the body in space. The Instrument for Intervention loft is designed to negotiate the move-ments of its two inhabitants within the limits of a small Manhattan loft space. Finally, Hybrid Cartographies recreates the complex trajectories of Seoul into an operable Möebius book/map, requiring one to unfold the map in order to read and navigate through the city. Each project engages the body and its material interfaces as a process of invention and intervention, articulating a material corpo-reality in an increasingly disembodied world.

>ACUPUNCTURE VEST

>The Acupuncture Vest takes as its site the body in pain. The project casts the space between the flatness of the acupressure point map and the contoured body. Blurring the distinction between landscapes and bodies, the project employs a MicroScribe digitizer to survey the body and produce a series of contours. The body landscape is filtered through the digital model and reproduced as a contoured mold for a rubber cast. The cast-rubber body-scape, filtered and defamiliarized through this process, is then mapped with a series of acupuncture pressure points. The Acupuncture Vest, the solid rubber casting of the space between the body and its two-dimensional map, is etched with the acupuncture template, allowing the user to operate on the body, collapsing the distinction of the acupuncturist, tailor, and surveyor.

>**below**_>Model of a female torso using a three-dimensional digitizer

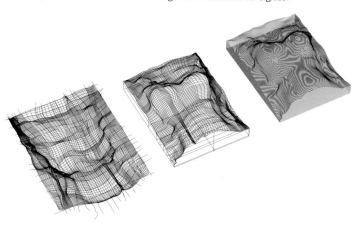

>**top**_>Plexiglass-laminated mold

>**center/right**_>Acupuncture points mapped on front vest elevation

>**center/left, bottom**_>View of vest

>**top**_>Torso sections for laminated mold

>**bottom**_>Plexiglass mold and rubber cast of the Acupuncture Vest

>**top**_>Surface transparency of Acupuncture Vest

>**bottom**_>Negative space of the torso with acupuncture points

>DEFENSIBLE DRESS

>The Defensible Dress is a response to the increasing breakdown and encroachment on personal space in everyday life. Historically, each culture and generation has had varying definitions of personal boundaries. Globalization and the urban condition have diminished an understanding of, and respect for, such space. Personal space is increasingly challenged and violated by external pressures. Inspired by the porcupine and the blowfish, the Defensible Dress marks the wearer's personal space, by activating a space-defining physical projection around the body. The extents of the personal space zone are defined as a numerical distance by the dress wearer. When infrared sensors detect an approaching body entering the personal space zone, a series of mechanical pines are activated, bristling to prevent encroachment into this space.

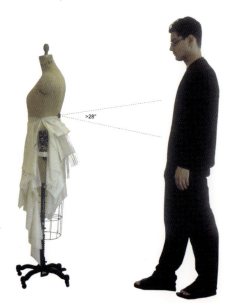

DISTANCE > SET PSD DISTANCE

>**top**_>BASIC Stamp microcontroller

>**bottom**_>Defensible Dress activated by an approaching body

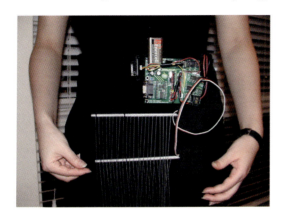

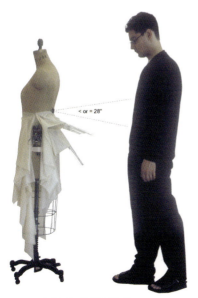

DISTANCE = SET PSD DISTANCE

DISTANCE < SET PSD DISTANCE

>INTERACTIVE PLEATED WALL

>The pleated wall prototype is a self-supporting structural surface and display wall. The homogenous surface becomes mutable. Its cuts, scores, and pleats allow for variegation in permeability—to view and to pass through. Its flexibility lies in its operable folds, which simultaneously imbue the almost two-dimensional wall with structural stability and textural unpredictability. Like a house of cards, the pleated wall celebrates its own planar improbability. Fabricated from an 1/8-inch aluminum plate, the pleated wall stabilizes itself through a pleating strategy. By hinging at its folds, the wall can expand and contract, subtly or abruptly, to depths ranging from 1/8th of an inch to 16 inches.

The continuity and discontinuity of the surface is made incrementally. The modules are fixed vertically and stacked through a series of notches. The panels stack and interlock to transfer their loads, stitching together a continuous surface. The pleated wall acts like a woven membrane where each unit gains structural stability from its adjacency to other panels. To accommodate different site conditions, the pleated wall is flexible. It can expand into shallow folds to cover larger areas with less depth or compress into more acute folds with greater depth, as required.

Installed at The Architectural League of New York, the Interactive Pleated Wall served as a display wall for the body of work under the title "emBodied Tectonics." Gaps between pleated panels were equipped with light tables to illuminate transparencies of the work. Infrared sensors were installed behind the wall to sense the presence of a viewing body. Aluminum rods, fitted through the perforations in the wall, would then retract with the presence of a viewer, creating an interactive space of display. The "inverse porcupine" wall invites the viewer into a relationship with the display, charting his or her movements across its surface.

>Electrical engineer: Matt Reynolds

>Fabrication assistance: Kyle Steinfeld, Tim Morshead, Amy Yang

>**top**_>Transformation of the Interactive Pleated Wall

>**center/left**_>Hinging study of one pleat unit

>**bottom**_>one-to-one mock up of one pleat unit

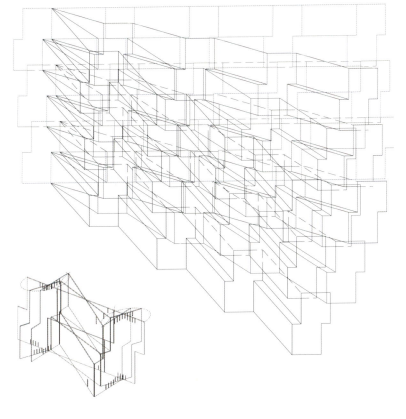

>**below+right**_>Stacking process of the pleated wall

>**top**_>Wall controller

>**bottom/left**_>Sensor-activated rods react to the presence of a viewing body

>**bottom/right**_>Wall controllers from the back side of the wall

>**below**_>Insertion of light tables in the gaps created by the folds

>BETWEEN BODIES AND WALLS

>Graduate Level Two Studio, Massachusetts Institute of Technology

>This design studio explores the mutability of material concepts as a means to inscribe, contain, and extend the body in space. Beginning with the body's own living container, the skin, students were asked to analyze and excavate a selection of second skins worn to clothe, protect, obscure, extend, enable, reveal, constrict, constrain, or enclose the body. Students were then asked to conceptualize, design, and fabricate a third skin—the walls, which were installed in a public hallway at MIT. An investigation into the thickness, materiality, and bodily engagement or occupancy of the wall initiated the tectonic speculation for the studio. This three-week, full-scale project created a series of interactive wall spaces that engaged, enclosed, and interacted with the public.

>**below**_>Wrist Guard, fiberglass study

 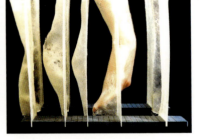

>Tim Morshead

>**left**_>Wall Building Wall, rubber mold model

>**right**_>Wall Building Wall, plaster cast of handheld mold

>Kyle Steinfeld and Amy Yang

>SHEAR WALL

>The tectonic interweaving of two semitransparent surfaces creates a self-supporting container/wall/screen, which pulls apart to allow one to occupy its thickness. The body's presence in the wall is registered as a deflection map on one surface of fiberglass and a transparency map on the opposing surface of steel.

>**below**_>Shear Wall, fiberglass and steel

>Meredith Atkinson and Tim Morshead

>**below**_>Shear Wall, fiberglass and steel

>FULL CONTACT ORIGAMI

>The relationship between the body and an architectural armor
is explored by creating two faceted and hinged surfaces. The
body, folding and unfolding, creates a dialog between the two
varying ranges of motion within these surface systems.

>**below**_>Full Contact Origami Wall, anodized aluminum and mesh

 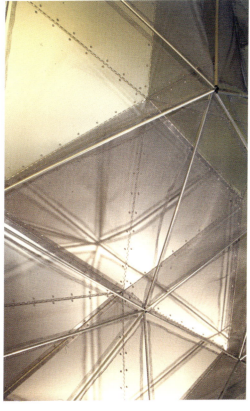

>Rebecca Luther and Tracy Taylor

>INSTRUMENT FOR INTERVENTION
>New York City

>This project is about three discrete interventions in an interior live/work space in Chelsea initiated by the space displaced by a baby grand piano. The clients requested three architectural instruments: a platform, a door, and a closet.

>The platform:

The platform acts as an elevated element between the floor and the ceiling, and serves as a small work area, a space for informal balcony seating, and a sleeping loft. The platform is hung in tension using a steel strap anchored to the ceiling structure. Folded hot-rolled steel plates are used to create the structural risers for the stair, allowing each tread to act as a cantilevered shelf.

>The door:

This studio apartment lacked a door between the public living area and the private bedroom area. The illegal "bedroom" at the back of the apartment had no exterior exposure—no access to light and air. The threshold between living and sleeping areas was further complicated by an awkwardly stepped soffit, as well as a main entry door in perpendicular adjacency. Negotiating these parameters, a set of interlocking operable doors allow light to filter from a window at the front of the apartment, straight through to the back of the bedroom. The two doors are set out of plane from each other, creating an interlocking framework that accommodates the soffit condition and marks the threshold between sleeping and living areas.

>The closet:

The closet acts as a window, light source, and storage space. The clients' wardrobes and storage areas are hidden behind the laminated glass sliding screens. The depth of the cabinetry is emphasized by the lighting, allowing the wall to act as a light box. The reflection on the surface of the wall gives the impression of spatial depth, bringing the city into the bedroom through its surface reflection.

>**left**_>The platform

>**center**_>The door

>**right**_>The closet

>**top**_>Suspended platform

>**bottom**_>Cantilevered stair detail

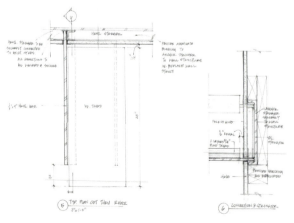

>**top**_>Tread and riser detail

>**bottom**_>Cantilevered stair detail

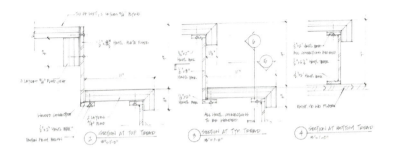

>**top/left+bottom_**>Artificial window: reflective and illuminated closet

>**top/right_**>Offset door detail

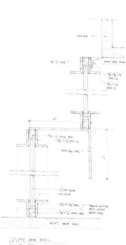

>**top**_>Hinged gap between the doors

>HYBRID CARTOGRAPHIES

>*Seoul's Consuming Spaces* is both a map and a detour. Like the city, it contains prescribed paths and open trajectories, allowing the reader to navigate as well as drift through specific sites of consumer spaces. This map/book is designed to juxtapose and unfold three different market/mall typologies, dating from premodernist, modernist, and postmodern periods. These sites are graphically and textually narrated from a historical, social, and spatial perspective. Designed as a series of intertwined paths, the reader navigates its multiple folds, discovering its textual paths.

The book is made through the manipulation of a single sheet of sixty-by-sixty-centimeter paper, printed on the front and back. It is offset-printed with just two plates, then cut and folded to produce the fifty pages in the book. The surface was cut spiraling inwards toward the center, then the surface was folded in alternate directions and closed by attaching the last module on the back side to the first module on the first side, creating a Möebius strip—a continuous loop without a clear inside and outside.

>**below_**>Layout of the unfolded book in the process of folding into final format

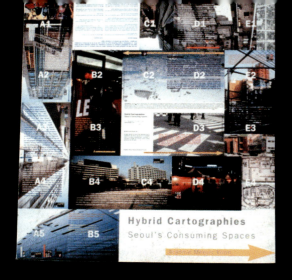

Hybrid Cartographies
Seoul's Consuming Spaces

>DZO ARCHITECTURE

>Many of the products we use and the spaces we inhabit are formed to fit into larger patterns of productions. Our projects challenge the machine as a template to deploy a greater degree of variation in the production process.

These projects are the consequences of a new formal freedom fostered by the development of digital technologies. The complex forms forced us to integrate manufacturing techniques as a primordial force in the design process. Computer numerically controlled devices allow us to move away from the mold of component-based construction. For example, the shape of the structure and lighting device of the Flemington Jewish Community Center is based on the mass production of nonstandard concrete panels.

The prototype becomes the product.

Another aspect of this work is the redefinition of the notion of surface. Projects like the Tenerife Passenger Terminal integrate the envelope of the building as a programmatic strategy in and of itself. Instead of the paradigmatic dissociation of modern architecture between structure and envelope, we are more interested in a fusion of structure and program akin to the way the interior skin of an airplane combines structure, storage, lighting, and air conditioning, or to the design of sport products made of layers with embedded functions such as breathability, water resistance, sensational cushioning, and shock absorption.

Our work on the dematerialization of spaces brought us closer to materiality and led us to better understand its impact on space and the alteration of our mental image of architecture.

>DOMESTIC TOPOGRAPHY

>Housing project and urban planning in Tenerife, Spain

>Site

>Located on the lower part of the Añaza development plan, the site of the competition is witness of two different conditions that left it isolated from the urban extension of Santa Cruz de Tenerife.

The first condition was the presence of a steep topography. The slope of the coast increases toward the sea as is shown in the road patterns. Moreover, a series of ravines create topographic discontinuities and limit the accessibility to the sea.

Secondly, the site, at the edge of two different urban development plans, was never integrated into a broader vision. Lacking spatial definition, the ravines were always considered a problematic frontier that existed between two parts of the urban development plans that ignored the area.

>Curving the edge

>Our project attempts to qualify the limit of the site by curving the edge of the ravine inside-in. The dwellings are spread out along the edge of the ravine, weaving between its two sides. Instead of erasing the topographic differences or smoothing the natural landscape, we enhanced the specificity of each side of the ravine in order to create a new urban condition. The difference of orientation and the steepness of the slope are specific elements of the landscape that predetermine a new relationship with a future urban environment. The southern ravine is an opportunity to create a programmatic transition from the upper part of Añaza to the sea: a mixture of housing, small offices or retail spaces on one side, and a public park, with sport and social facilities, on the other one. These latter open spaces become a future greenscape filled with public facilities linking the plateau of Añaza to the sea. Our proposal defines

>**below**_>Urban plan

the site in the slope as a new urban system interacting with the plateau of Añaza rather than being a mere extension of it.

>Domestic topography

>Between landscape and urban structure the screens suggest a virtual envelope of the dwellings, a spine of growth and extension.

At the scale of the building, the screens are defined as an interface between inside and outside space, between private and public spaces. They also filter the sun and the wind, and frame the view to the horizon. The wood shades of the screens can be unfolded individually along the facade to open the view to the sea; the landscape will therefore register a domestic topography. The project reveals the ravine as a scenic and unique moment of the Santa Cruz coastline and articulates different sequences of urban space.

>Urban landscaping

>The site is free of any construction. The project negotiates between urban environment and landscape, between living spaces and the brutality of the topography. It creates a new topography by vertically stitching the edge of the ravine on one side and by carving out the landscape on the other side.

The housing project is conceived as urban strips following the lines of the existing topography. These strips are accessible by public decks, playing with the profile of the slope and leading to the dwellings along a wood screen of variable density. These public platforms link hybrid programs and draw a unique urban sequence from the basalt outflows to the tropical vegetation to the infinite horizon of the ocean.

>Model photography: Anne Sophie Restoux

>**top**_>Study model of housing screen

>**center**_>View of landscape decks

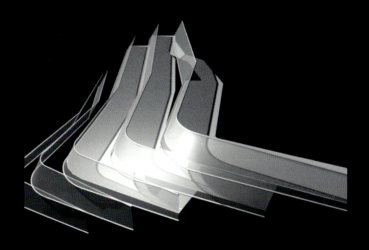

>**below**_>Floor plan of landscape decks

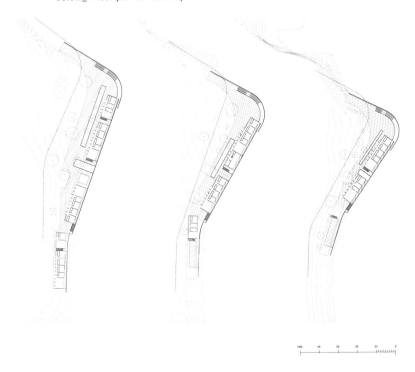

>**top**_>Scale model photography

>**bottom**_>Axonometry of housing system

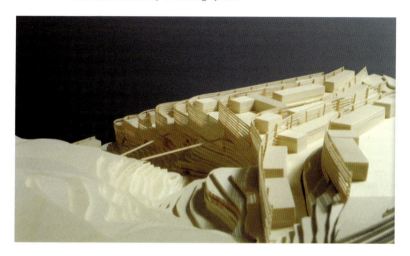

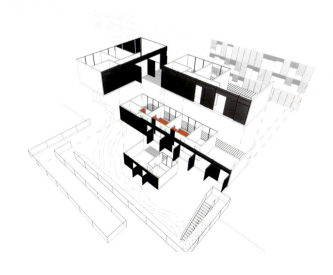

>**top**_>Transversal section of housings

>**bottom**_>Plan of housing units

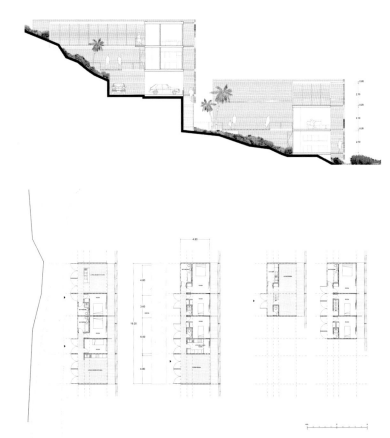

>**below**_>View of housing screens

>ASC PROJECT

>Concert hall in Sarajevo

>*Libre-Jeu*

>The ASC (altered state of consciousness) Project is less an apology for complexity than a critique of a certain panographic architecture, that is to say, an architecture that is already exhausted by its planar right angle representation. It does not downplay comprehension, but makes the senses vibrate in curved trajectories. Our exploration is based upon the simple pleasure of music lovers—closing one's eyes and leaving oneself to be carried away by a symphony.

   The building integrates itself in the site, a preliminary topographical alteration that allows public service spaces to slide from underneath (lower lobby access, cafeteria, and library) to above the natural ground level (the restaurant). The double facade in etched glass is conceived as a filter, a superposition of two grids of horizontal lines that mask and blur the complex relations of the interior surfaces. This spectral logic is reinforced by the architectural definition of these elements. The translucent resin surfaces, lighted from the interior, flow from the ramps to the wall, all up to the inner decorative paneling in the concert halls, creating surface tension and hierarchical contradictions. Rather than a mere wall, the limit between the performance space and the ramps, or the ramps and the foyers, twists and doubles over on itself in a process of thickening the line to a space. The edge of the performance hall and the outer layer of the ramps blend together in a new set of continuities between circulation pattern and acoustical reverberation.

   The stage layout of each auditorium responds to this process, searching for a fluidity between the circulation of the balcony and the geometry of the acoustics in the hall. The plaster panels that enclose each of the auditoriums pleat themselves, forming curious surfaces, reproducing the same motif of amplification and transformation developed in the alteration of the project's ground surface.

By reflecting the relationship between circulation, ground, and building envelope in a movement that redefines the motion of limit, the project unfolds. A *Libre-Jeu* of un-limitations that suspend for an instant the weight of measure: the space of the blink of an eye.

>Project team: DZO and A. Carbone and S. Ray. Structural engineer: Ove Arup. Model: J. L. Courtois

>**below**_>View of foyer

>**below**_>Aerial perspective of building

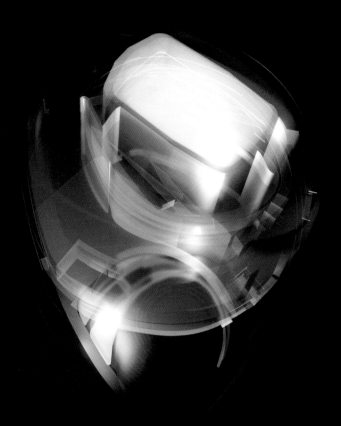

>**top**_>Plan of main concert hall

>**bottom**_>Ramp system around the concert hall

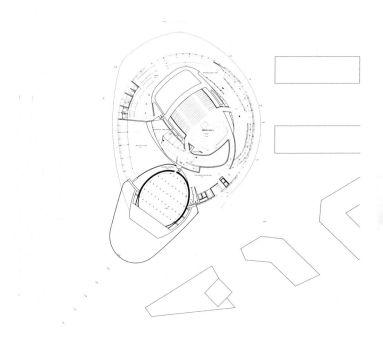

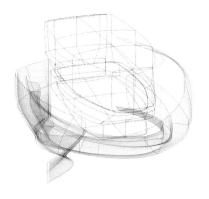

>(UN)-SCRIPTING
>Flemington Jewish Community Center, New Jersey

>Text and Judaism
>The reading and interpretation of the Torah has been for generations the touchstone act of Jewish religious life. The structure of a Talmud page reveals the importance of interpretation of the holy text: A quote from the Mishna (the foundational commentary on the Bible and Jewish law) occupies the center of the page. It is a layered textual structure conducive to the addition of ideas, understandings, and analysis by commentators through the years.

>Anamorphic signs
>Hebrew calligraphy is a generative force in the design of the synagogue. The letters shape the space, limiting and altering the threshold between interiority and exteriority. These anamorphic objects express the graphic singularity of the Hebrew alphabet projected within the building spaces. On the facade the Hebrew letters engender a vibration of meaning in a movement from reading to interpretation, from word to deed, fostering an unceasing blurring of text and space at different levels within the project.

>Light Inversion
>The synagogue, the social hall, and the school are wrapped in an envelope perforated by Hebrew text. The synagogue's facade is an

assembly of composite panels of wood and frosted glass. Cutouts in the wood allow the light to go through the panel and project the shapes of letters on the translucent panel inside. During the day the letters appear with different degrees of sharpness and color inside the sanctuary depending on the exterior light conditions. At dusk when the Shabbat begins, the light of the sanctuary reveals, to the outside, the writing on the facade.

The Shema is inscribed on the walls of the building, expressing the centrality of the text in the Jewish tradition and the command-ment to "write them [it] on the doorposts of your homes and upon your gates." In our design the words are freed from their encase-ment in the Mezuzah and become an integral part of the building, inscribed and wrapped around its wall.

>With the participation of Esther Sperber

>Model: B. Isambert. Architect of record: Hunt Architects

>**top**_>Manipulation of Hebraic calligraphy

>**bottom+left**_>Typographic hybrid

>**below**_>Floor plan

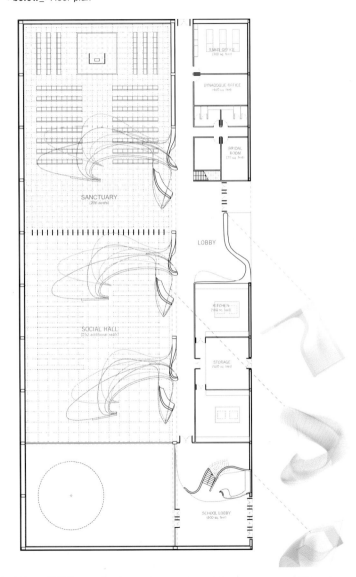

>**top_**>Prototypes of synagogue structure

>**bottom_**>Axonometry of synagogue structure

>**top**_>Section trough sanctuary

>**bottom**_>Front elevation of sanctuary

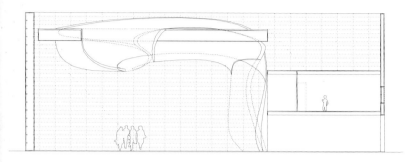

NORTH ELEVATION

>**below**_>Interior view of sanctuary

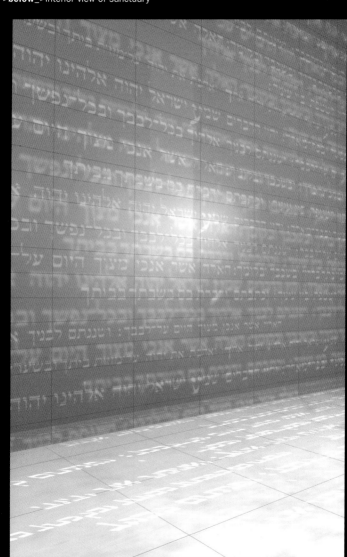

>FORMS OF EXTERIORITY

>Passenger terminal in Santa Cruz de Tenerife Harbor, Spain

>Located in the Santa Cruz de Tenerife Harbor, this passenger terminal project consists of the integration of harbor activities with specific conditions (accesses, road connections, road services, heavy vehicles transit, docks, passenger loading and unloading) with the city seafront. This integration is a mix of recreational, commercial, and entertainment areas with densities that need to be defined. The programmatic organization we developed aimed to reach a critical mass of activities (retail, restaurants, entertainment, offices, and sport facilities) so that the terminal could function as a whole.

>Time-activation landscapes
>The occupancy of the existing pier fluctuates tremendously during the day. The schedule of departure and arrival of boats and ferries on the site regulates the flow of people, buses, and taxis on the site. Using a fluid simulation technology, these paths were modeled to reveal zones of the site activated at different times: the time-activation landscapes.

The site is seen as a milieu of homogeneous consistency transmitting uniform forces. The existing programs at the edge of the site affect each point of this field like a series of waves where the amplitude decreases with the distance.

>see p. 172/173

>**below**_>Panoramic view of the pier and the city

>Programmatic flows

>The programs were thus organized in relation to a schedule rather than in terms of spatial proximities, exploring new possibilities of the use of the infrastructure.

This dynamic system expands, in a way, the concept of phase diagram to the notion of delay strategy. The new programs are then seen as a strategy to reschedule the movement of passengers through the terminal by delaying or accelerating it.

>Y structure

>The programmatic layer is materialized as a set of variable sectional conditions along the edges of the pier. Y-shaped steel beams intertwine and are used to accommodate the slopes of the ramp, leading cars and pedestrians to the different levels of the structure. It also allows the height of the terminal floors to be adjusted to the different loading heights of boats and ferries.

>Model: Kennedy Fabrications. Structural engineer: ADC Structures/ Jean-Marc Weil, Paris

>**right**_>Flow analysis map

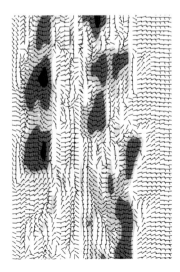

>**below+right**_>Activation maps of the site generated by a field analysis, revealing singular patterns of organization

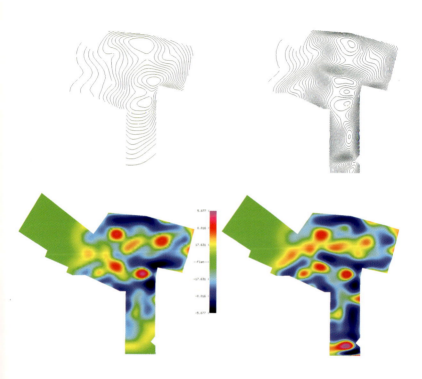

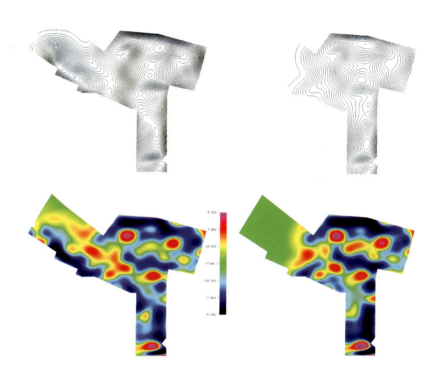

>**top/left_**>Analysis of weekly schedule of boats and ferries

>**center_**>Sectional conditions from the city to the sea

>**bottom_**>Structural principle of section showing the Y aluminum beams

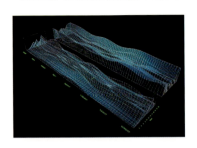

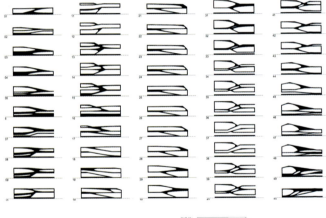

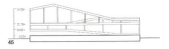

>**below**_>Structural model of passenger terminal

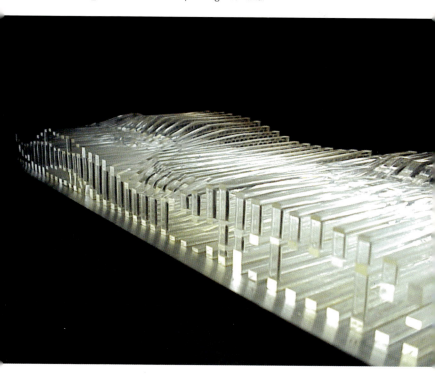

>End.